The Treaty
of Versailles

MILESTONES
IN MODERN
WORLD HISTORY

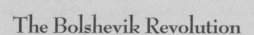

MILESTONES
IN MODERN
WORLD HISTORY

500 · · · 1750 · ·   · · · 1940 · · · 2000

The Treaty
of Versailles

LOUISE CHIPLEY SLAVICEK

CHELSEA HOUSE
PUBLISHERS
An imprint of Infobase Publishing

The Treaty of Versailles

Copyright © 2010 by Infobase Publishing

All rights reserved. No part of this book may be reproduced or utilized in any form or by any means, electronic or mechanical, including photocopying, recording, or by any information storage or retrieval systems, without permission in writing from the publisher. For information, contact:

Chelsea House
An imprint of Infobase Publishing
132 West 31st Street
New York, NY 10001

Library of Congress Cataloging-in-Publication Data

Slavicek, Louise Chipley, 1956–
The Treaty of Versailles / Louise Chipley Slavicek.
  p. cm. — (Milestones in modern world history)
Includes bibliographical references and index.
ISBN 978-1-60413-277-9 (hardcover)
1. Treaty of Versailles (1919)—Juvenile literature. 2. Paris Peace Conference (1919-1920)—Juvenile literature. 3. World War, 1914-1918—Peace—Juvenile literature. I. Title.

D644.S58 2009
940.3'141—dc22   2008054804

Chelsea House books are available at special discounts when purchased in bulk quantities for businesses, associations, institutions, or sales promotions. Please call our Special Sales Department in New York at (212) 967-8800 or (800) 322-8755.

You can find Chelsea House on the World Wide Web at http://www.chelseahouse.com.

Text design by Erik Lindstrom
Cover design by Alicia Post
Composition by Keith Trego
Cover printed by Yurchak Printing, Landisville, Pa.
Book printed and bound by Yurchak Printing, Landisville, Pa.
Printed in the United States of America

This book is printed on acid-free paper.

All links and Web addresses were checked and verified to be correct at the time of publication. Because of the dynamic nature of the Web, some addresses and links may have changed since publication and may no longer be valid.

CONTENTS

"Easier to Make War than Peace"

A round 10 minutes past five on the morning of November 11, 1918, German delegates signed an armistice with their Allied conquerors in a quiet forest glen near Compiègne, France. As news of the cease-fire spread, people poured into the streets across Europe and America to celebrate the end of more than four years of bitter fighting between the Allies, led by France, Great Britain, and the United States, and the Central Powers, led by Germany. Waving flags, belting out patriotic songs, and pounding on pots and pans, they paraded and danced through the streets of Paris, London, New York, and countless other cities and towns across the globe. The joyful crowds were relieved that the bloodletting—which had claimed the lives of an estimated 10 million troops since the outbreak of the Great War (as World War I was then called) in 1914—had ended. They were also optimistic that a new era of understanding and harmony among nations was about to begin.

THE COMPLEX AND CONTROVERSIAL PROCESS OF PEACEMAKING

In January 1919, two months after the German armistice went into effect, delegates from nearly three dozen Allied nations spanning six continents gathered in Paris to try to fashion a lasting peace for the postwar world. The number of difficult issues facing the Paris Peace Conference was daunting. Delegates not only had to discuss complex and sensitive territorial, financial, and military terms for Germany and its World War I allies, but they also had to redraw the maps of Eastern and Central Europe and the Middle East, in the wake of the wartime collapse of the vast Austro-Hungarian, Russian, and Turkish Ottoman empires. This task was greatly complicated by long-standing ethnic and religious resentments and rivalries among the inhabitants of these regions.

It required six months for the Paris Conference's top delegates—President Woodrow Wilson of the United States, Premier Georges Clemenceau of France, Prime Minister David Lloyd George of Great Britain, and Prime Minister Vittorio Orlando of Italy—to hammer out the 438 articles of the settlement with the Allies' principal opponent in the war, Germany. Since each of the so-called Big Four had arrived in Paris with different and frequently contradictory visions and agendas for the postwar world, their almost daily meetings during the winter and spring of 1919 were often fraught with tension. Late in the negotiations, Orlando became so irate with his colleagues over a territorial question involving Italy that he stormed out of the conference and refused to return for nearly two weeks. "It is much easier," Clemenceau concluded wryly, "to make war than peace."[1]

Besides devising a peace settlement for Germany, the Paris negotiators had to contend with a wide range of other

The Big Four—British Prime Minister David Lloyd George, Italian President Vittorio Orlando, French Prime Minister Georges Clemenceau, and U.S. President Woodrow Wilson—at the Hotel Crillon in Paris, just prior to the Versailles Peace Conference.

territorial, financial, and military questions arising from the Great War. The Big Four were also laying the groundwork for separate treaties with each of Berlin's wartime allies: Austria, Hungary, Bulgaria, and Turkey. Some of the agreements, like the Treaty of St. Germain with Austria, were completed and approved rather quickly. Others, particularly the Turkish peace settlement, took a great deal more time to conclude. Indeed, the final peace agreement with Turkey would not be signed until July 24, 1923, a little more than four years after the Treaty of Versailles, the first and by far the most famous of the Allied peace treaties, was signed with Germany.

Historians have generally come down hard on the Allied peacemakers for many perceived diplomatic and moral failings. Nearly a century after the end of World War I, the justice and fundamental wisdom of the treaties they devised, particularly the Treaty of Versailles with Germany, are still being debated. In recent years, however, scholars have become more sympathetic to the plight of the Paris negotiators as they grappled with the complex political, economic, and security dilemmas confronting the world following the most destructive war to date. "If they could have done better," writes Margaret MacMillan, one of the Peace Conference's most recent and respected chroniclers, "they certainly could have done much worse."[2]

The Roots of World War I

On June 28, 1914, exactly five years to the day before the signing of the peace treaty at the Palace of Versailles in France, the heir to the throne of the Austro-Hungarian Empire was assassinated in Sarajevo, Bosnia. Austrian Archduke Franz Ferdinand's murder at the hands of a Serbian nationalist is generally considered the spark that ignited World War I. Yet the roots of the devastating four-year struggle stretched back much further than the summer of 1914. By the time armed hostilities broke out between the Central Powers of Germany and Austria-Hungary and the Allied Powers of Russia, France, and Great Britain in early August, Europe had been preparing for a major war for more than two decades. All the chief European nations had increased their spending on armaments, signed defensive alliances with other countries, and, with the exception of Great Britain, passed national conscription (military draft) laws. Historians agree that the single most important factor behind the escalating tension of the late 1800s and early 1900s was the emergence in 1871 of a formidable new military, political, and economic power in the heart of the continent: the German Empire.

THE RISE OF THE GERMAN EMPIRE

Before 1871, Germany consisted of a loosely knit confederation of more than three dozen self-ruling principalities, duchies (areas ruled by a duke or duchess), and free cities. The two largest and most influential states in the German Confederation were the militaristic kingdom of Prussia in the east and the Austrian Empire (reorganized in 1867 as the Dual Monarchy of Austria-Hungary) in the south. By the mid-1800s, nationalism—devotion to the interests and culture of one's nation or ethnic community—had taken hold among central Europe's German-speaking people, many of whom began to clamor for the creation of a united Germany. Eager to guarantee the influence of their own state within a politically unified Germany, the governments of Prussia and Austria competed for control of the burgeoning unification movement. In 1866, under the skillful direction of Prime Minister Otto von Bismarck, Prussia routed the Austrians on the battlefield and forced them out of the German Confederation altogether. Five years later, the Prussian army achieved a stunning military victory against another longtime rival, France, in the Franco-Prussian War. In January 1871, Prussian King Wilhelm I, taking advantage of the unprecedented patriotic fervor that the war aroused among Germans, proclaimed the creation of a unified German Reich (empire) at the magnificent Palace of Versailles near Paris with himself as its first kaiser (emperor). A few months later, French officials signed a humiliating peace treaty with the kaiser's new government in Berlin. Under the settlement's harsh terms, France was required to pay reparations of 5 billion gold francs and cede its eastern province of Alsace and part of the neighboring province of Lorraine to the Reich. (Reparations are compensation in money or materials exacted from a defeated nation by the victors for war-related damages and expenses.)

The new Reich grew at a breathtakingly rapid pace from its founding in 1871 at Versailles until the outbreak of World War I in 1914. By the first years of the twentieth century, Germany boasted one of the globe's most dynamic economies and had replaced Great Britain as the foremost industrial nation in Europe. From 1890 to 1913, historian Alan Sharp notes,

> [Germany's] population increased from 49 to 66 millions, the output of her coal mines grew from 89 to 277 million tons, while her steel production of 17.6 million tons in 1913 was greater than the combined total of Britain, France, and Russia. . . . In chemical and electrical goods Germany led the world, and her young, vigorous, and rapidly expanding population was well-educated, providing intelligent recruits for her industries and powerful armies.[1]

Under the direction of Wilhelm's ambitious and militaristic son, Wilhelm II, who reigned as kaiser from 1888 to 1918, the Reich used its vast wealth, industrial resources, and technological expertise to build its army into one of the best-equipped and most efficient force on the globe. As part of his quest to boost German prestige in Europe and throughout the world, Wilhelm II also sought to create an overseas colonial empire for Germany, just as many European nations had done in the late nineteenth and early twentieth centuries. By 1914, Germany had secured valuable territories and economic concessions in Asia, Africa, and the Pacific to the dismay of its imperialist competitors in those regions, including France, Russia, and the world's leading colonial power, Great Britain.

Aside from friction over competing colonial and commercial interests, another critical source of tension between the

German Reich and its neighbors centered on the issue of military alliances. Anxious to strengthen his nation's security on the continent, German Chancellor Otto von Bismarck negotiated the Triple Alliance in 1882 with Italy, which had also recently undergone political unification, and Prussia's old nemesis, Austria-Hungary. According to the terms of the defensive alliance, the three members were obliged to aid one another in the event of an attack by two or more countries. By the mid-1890s, Germany boasted Europe's premier land force and was set to embark on an ambitious program of naval expansion that would soon make its fleet the second largest in the world after Great Britain's. Deeply concerned about Germany's growing military clout and what the shifting balance of power in Europe might mean for their countries, longtime foes France and Russia put aside their differences and signed their own defensive alliance. Under the provisions of the new Franco-Russian Alliance, each nation pledged military assistance in the event of an attack by Germany or another Triple Alliance member backed by Germany. Preferring to maintain a policy of "splendid isolation" from the continent, the last of the great European powers, Great Britain, had long shied away from international alliances. Yet, uneasy about Germany's mounting military might and particularly its impressive new naval fleet, Britain's leaders decided to break with tradition and join Russia and France in a protective association dubbed the Triple Entente in 1907. According to the loosely worded agreement, Britain was not actually obliged to go to war in defense of France or Russia. Nonetheless, the creation of the Triple Entente effectively divided Europe into two opposing and increasingly wary armed camps.

THE UNSTABLE BALKANS

Political instability and rivalry in the Balkans, the easternmost of Europe's three major southern peninsulas, further complicated the already strained relationships among the great powers in the years leading up to World War I. For centuries, three empires—the Turkish Ottoman, the Russian, and the Austrian—had competed for supremacy in the mountainous and ethnically diverse region. Following its defeat by a coalition of independent Balkan nations including Serbia, Greece, and Bulgaria in 1912, however, the tottering Ottoman Empire lost virtually all its territory in the Balkans.

With the Ottomans gone, Austria-Hungary, Russia, and the Kingdom of Serbia (the Balkan nation that had obtained the most new territory from the vanquished Ottoman Empire), emerged as the three main powers on the peninsula.

The biggest of the various ethnic groups who populated the Balkans, and the predominant group within Serbia, were the Slavs. Even before the war of 1912 with Turkey, Serbia's rulers had dreamed of expanding their kingdom's territory and influence within the Balkans. They were encouraged by Russia, the world's largest Slavic nation and the self-proclaimed protector of Slavs everywhere. To accomplish this goal, the Serbian government in Belgrade wanted to bring together other southern Slavs in a new Balkan state under Serbian leadership. Serbia's neighbor to the west, the Austro-Hungarian province of Bosnia, was of particular interest to the little kingdom's nationalistic rulers since it was home to large numbers of Slavs of Serbian descent. Austria-Hungary, which had been struggling for years to contain growing discontent among Slavs and other ethnic minorities throughout its sprawling European empire, worried about this development. In fact, by 1908 the Dual Monarchy of Austria-Hungary was not only concerned about Serbia's intentions in Bosnia but also in the adjacent Austro-Hungarian province of Herzegovina. Resolved to sending Serbia and its ally Russia a message about preserving Austro-Hungarian influence in the Balkans, the Dual Monarchy announced that the empire was formally annexing the provinces of Bosnia and Herzegovina that year.

The Dual Monarchy's annexation of Bosnia and Herzegovina, however, left Serbia more determined than ever to "liberate" its neighbors from the sway of their non-Slavic rulers in Vienna and Budapest. While Belgrade lodged a formal protest against the annexation, a small group of Serbian nationalists, including several renegade army officers, vowed to take more drastic action. Determined to drive the Dual Monarchy out of Bosnia and Herzegovina entirely and absorb the two provinces into a "Greater Serbia," they formed a secret terrorist society, the Black Hand, and began to plot assassinations of Austro-Hungarian officials in the Balkans. By 1914, the Black Hand had several hundred members and was ready to carry out its most daring mission to date: the assassination of the presumed heir to the Austro-Hungarian throne, Archduke Franz Ferdinand, the nephew of 83-year-old Emperor Franz Josef.

THE ASSASSINATION OF FRANZ FERDINAND AND THE OUTBREAK OF THE GREAT WAR

In early June 1914, after learning that Franz Ferdinand had scheduled a state visit to the Bosnian capital of Sarajevo later that month, the Black Hand's leaders decided to recruit and train several young Bosnian nationalists to kill the archduke. Among the youthful death squad was Gavrilo Princip, a 19-year-old student of Slavic-Serbian ancestry. On the morning of June 28, the terrorist approached Franz Ferdinand's stopped car and shot the archduke and his wife, Sophie, at point-blank range with a revolver given to him by his contacts in the Black Hand.

News of the Austrian royal couple's murder was greeted with sympathy and indignation throughout Europe. Sympathy for the Dual Monarchy soon turned to alarm, however, when it became clear that the Austro-Hungarian government intended to use the killings as an excuse to go after its competitor in the western Balkans, Serbia. Although there was no evidence that the Serbian government was involved in the archduke's death, Austro-Hungarian leaders publicly accused Belgrade of masterminding the assassination. A little more than three weeks after the shootings, on July 23, 1914, the Dual Monarchy

The assassination of Archduke Franz Ferdinand, heir to the Austro-Hungarian throne, and his wife, Sophie, on June 28, 1914, precipitated World War I. Here, the archduke's assassin, Gavrilo Princip, is arrested moments after the shooting.

formally presented Serbia with a list of 10 harsh and humiliating demands as punishment for its alleged complicity in Franz Ferdinand's death. Acceptance of the ultimatum would effectively turn Serbia into a satellite of the Dual Monarchy. Still, fearful of the combined military might of Austria-Hungary and its powerful ally, Germany, Belgrade agreed to nine of the demands and asked that the remaining one be submitted to an international conference for arbitration. To the shock of most observers in Europe, the Austro-Hungarian government flatly rejected Serbia's conciliatory offer and severed all diplomatic relations on July 25. Three days later, Austria-Hungary declared war on the Balkan kingdom.

Apparently hoping to call Austria-Hungary's bluff, Czar Nicholas II of Russia warned the Dual Monarchy that unless it withdrew its forces from Serbian territory, Russian troops would begin to mobilize. Austro-Hungarian officials declined to back down. On July 31, the czar, determined to honor a defensive alliance Russia had signed with Serbia years earlier, reluctantly began the slow process of calling up Russia's massive but poorly organized army. The following day the Great War officially erupted: The German government, having quickly mobilized its own army, declared war on Russia, ostensibly to stop the czar from interfering in the dispute between Germany's ally, Austria-Hungary, and Serbia.

Over the next two weeks, the conflict spread across Europe as the continent's various military alliance systems sprang into action. On August 3, France called up its troops in a show of support for its ally, Russia. Using French mobilization as an excuse, Germany declared war on the French Republic that same day and immediately launched a massive preemptive strike against its old enemy delivered through the small, neutral nation of Belgium. On August 4, Great Britain—which along with the other leading European powers had signed an agreement decades earlier guaranteeing Belgium's right to remain neutral—declared war on Germany. On August 6, under pressure from Germany, the Dual Monarchy declared war on Russia; six days later France and Great Britain declared war on Austria-Hungary. Every one of the major European powers had now entered the conflict except the Kingdom of Italy, which decided to remain neutral. According to the government in Rome, the kingdom's obligations toward Germany and Austria under the Triple Alliance only required Italy to come to their aid if either country was attacked first. Yet far from being defensive, the struggle in which Berlin and Vienna were engaged was "a war of aggression" initiated by the Germans and Austrians themselves, Italian officials asserted.[2]

WHO STARTED WORLD WAR I? THE CONTROVERSIAL ISSUE OF GERMAN WAR GUILT

The question of who was to blame for the outbreak of war in August 1914 has been one of the frequently debated topics of modern history. One chief reason for this debate centers on the Paris Peace Conference itself. In a formal report to the conference in January 1919, the English, French, and American members of the Peace Conference's "Commission on the Responsibility of the Authors of the War" proclaimed that the war was clearly "premeditated" by the chief Central Power, Germany, in 1914 and "was the result of acts deliberately committed in order to make it unavoidable."[3] Six months later, the Allied framers of the Treaty of Versailles enshrined their view of the war's origins in Article 231 of the document, popularly dubbed the "war-guilt clause." According to the article, the Great War was "imposed upon them [the Allied Powers] by the aggression of Germany and her allies."[4]

Unsurprisingly, this portrayal of Germany as the war's villainous instigator created enormous resentment among Germans, particularly as Article 231 would be used by the Versailles Treaty's creators to justify the collection of reparations from them. Yet it was not only the Germans who disputed the Versailles version of how the Great War came about. Beginning in the 1920s, scholars from the United States and other Western nations also began to question the Peace Conference's claim that the bloody conflict had been "imposed upon" Russia, France, and the other Allied Powers by German aggression.

American historian Sidney Fay was one of the most outspoken and influential critics of the Allied verdict that Germany was responsible for the First World War. According to Fay's 1928 book, *The Origins of the World War*, all the great European powers shared the blame for the war's outbreak. Berlin, Fay maintained, had no intention of launching a general European war during the summer of 1914. The single most important cause of the Great War, he argued, was the interlocking web of defensive alliances in which all of the major European nations were enmeshed by the early twentieth century.

"ALL ROADS LEAD TO BERLIN"

Fay's contention that the Great War was the collective responsibility of the leading European nations quickly gained acceptance among scholars and the public alike. By the mid-twentieth century, it had become the standard version of the war's origins on both sides of the Atlantic. Then in 1961, more than three decades after the publication of *The Origins of the World War*, German historian Fritz Fischer unexpectedly reopened the war-guilt debate in *Grab for World Power*, an explosive 900-page study of Germany's role in World War I. Based on new evidence from previously unpublished government and military documents in Germany and Austria, Fischer asserted that, during the summer of 1914, the Reich's military and political leaders deliberately transformed what might have remained a localized dispute in the Balkans into a general European war. They accomplished this, he argued, by quietly egging on a reluctant Austria-Hungary to invade Serbia in July 1914, knowing that Russia was likely to come to the aid of its smaller Slavic ally and France to the defense of its chief European ally, Russia. Berlin's motive in engineering a general war in 1914, Fischer believed, was an overriding desire for European and even world domination. According to Fischer's interpretation, the Reich's ambitious leaders reasoned that, once the armies of its major rivals on the continent, Russia and France, had been routed, Germany could seize large amounts of valuable new territory in Europe as well as overseas.

After a separation spanning almost 50 years, East and West Germany were reunited in 1990 and long-hidden documents uncovered in East Germany lent support to

Fischer's—and the Paris peacemakers'—assertion that the Reich government was primarily to blame for starting World War I. According to historian David Fromkin's recent study, *Europe's Last Summer: Who Started the Great War in 1914?*, most scholars now agree that Germany pushed a vacillating Austria-Hungary into a violent confrontation with Serbia in late July 1914, fully realizing that this belligerent course of action was likely to trigger a larger war involving Russia and France. During the tense weeks following Franz Ferdinand's assassination, Fromkin writes, "Germany did not blindly back up Austria in its aggressiveness; on the contrary, it *led* Austria into aggressiveness and ordered it to go further and faster."[5] Historians Robin Prior, Trevor Wilson, and John Keegan agree with that assessment in their 1999 study, *The First World War*: "In comprehending the eruption of July 1914, all roads lead to Berlin."[6]

Regarding the question of why Berlin was willing—even eager—to incite a general war in Europe in July and August 1914, however, most contemporary scholars reject Fischer's argument that German leaders were motivated by a desire to conquer vast new territories. Fear, not ambition, was behind Berlin's stance, they assert. German leaders had long worried that the Reich's massive neighbor to the east, Russia, posed a grave potential threat to its economic position in Europe as well as its national security. By 1914, the populous yet notoriously backward Russian Empire had finally begun to make major strides in modernizing and expanding its industrial base, armed forces, and railroad system. At the same time, France—Russia's closest ally and Germany's bitter foe since the Franco-Prussian War (1870–1871)—was strengthening its own army. Having convinced themselves that a German-Russian showdown was inevitable, German political and military leaders believed it would be more advantageous to the Reich if that confrontation occurred sooner rather than later, before Russia and France had a chance to become more formidable opponents.

According to the Reich's long-standing war plan, the Schlieffen Plan, to win a conflict against Russia and France, the imperial army had to conduct a carefully timed two-front war in the east and the west. German troops must deliver a swift knockout blow to France's ground forces first, the Schlieffen Plan dictated, before turning their attention eastward toward Russia's slower-moving but much larger army. In Chief of Staff Helmuth von Moltke's updated version of the plan, the bulk of the German army would invade France at the nation's least fortified and therefore most vulnerable spot—its northeastern frontier with Belgium. While German troops fought their way to the French capital at Paris, Austria-Hungary would help to hold off any Russian advances toward Germany's eastern frontier. Once Paris had been secured and the French army routed, German forces could concentrate on Russia and the Eastern Front. As long as the German army was able to move forward swiftly with its two-front war plan, Moltke and his top generals were convinced that the Reich could achieve success in both the west and the east in a matter of months.

During the first heady weeks of the war, the Germans were not the only ones who anticipated a quick victory. The Reich's Allied opponents were also feeling optimistic. In August 1914, jubilant, flag-waving crowds gathered in cities and towns across Great Britain, France, Russia, Germany, and Austria-Hungary to cheer their departing troops. Few could have imagined then that what was supposed to have been a short and glorious contest would last four agonizing years, leaving 10 million soldiers dead and another 20 million wounded.

A War to
End All Wars

Within a month of the outbreak of hostilities on August
1, 1914, hopes for a swift victory had faded in both the
Central and Allied camps. On August 30, German troops beat
back an invading Russian army at Tannenberg in the Reich's
northeastern corner in a devastating rout that left more than
100,000 Russians dead or captured. But if the Allies had reason
to feel discouraged by developments on the Eastern Front in late
August, their morale was certainly boosted after Germany suffered a stunning setback on the Western Front in France, just
days after its triumph in the Battle of Tannenberg.

STALEMATE AND THE HUNT FOR NEW ALLIES
At first, Germany's military campaign in the West had gone
well. After fighting their way through Belgium, German troops

had swept into France and were headed toward the capital by mid-August. On September 5, however, French forces halted the main German advance toward Paris in the Marne River valley, about 30 miles (48 kilometers) east of the city. Following several days of fierce combat between the kaiser's troops and a combined Franco-British army, the Battle of the Marne ended in a decisive victory for the Allies. By September 10, the Germans had been forced to retreat as far north as the Aisne River near the French-Belgian border. There they embedded themselves in a series of interlocking, six- to eight-foot-deep (1.8- to 2.4-meter-deep) trenches as protection from the advancing French and British. When the Allies realized that they could not penetrate the heavily fortified German line, they began to dig out their own trenches. By the end of 1914, an elaborate network of German and Allied trenches stretched from Switzerland through Belgium and northeastern France all the way to the North Sea. For the next three years, the Western Front would remain virtually stationary as the Allies and Germans assailed their entrenched opponents with long-range artillery, aerial bombs, and poison gas in a grisly contest of attrition to determine which side could afford to lose the most men.

Although trench warfare never took hold on the Eastern Front, where vast open spaces gave armies plenty of room to maneuver, the fighting there had also degenerated into a stalemate by late 1914. With the bulk of its army stalled in Belgium and France, Germany was unable to transfer enough troops eastward to overcome the poorly equipped but massive Russian army. Moreover, Germany's ally Austria-Hungary was proving of limited value in the Eastern campaign. The Dual Monarchy's ineptly led troops could not even manage to defeat the small Serbian army, let alone make any significant headway against Russia's far bigger force.

As it became clear that, despite appallingly high casualty rates, neither side was likely to achieve a decisive victory anytime soon, securing additional allies became a priority for both

Trench warfare was a key element of the fighting in World War I. Pictured here is a German machine gun company in position near Darkehmen, Masuria, at the First Battle of the Masurian Lakes in September 1914.

sides. From late 1914 to 1916, the two opposing coalitions managed to enlist several new allies in Europe, the Middle East, and even East Asia. On the Allied side, these included Romania and Japan, who used the war as an excuse to seize German territories in China and the Pacific, and on the Central side, Bulgaria. The most important Central and Allied recruits during this period, however, were the Ottoman Empire, which had had long enjoyed close economic and military ties with the Reich, and the Kingdom of Italy. In October 1914, less than three months after the German invasion of Belgium launched World War I, the Ottoman Empire took up arms for the Central

Powers. Italy, by contrast, would prove considerably slower in relinquishing its neutrality to join the Allied Powers.

THE TREATY OF LONDON AND ITALY'S ENTRY INTO THE WAR

From the beginning of the fighting, the Allies and Germany vigorously competed for the support of Italy because of its long, central Mediterranean coastline as well as its proximity to Austria-Hungary. "Both Britain and France," Joe H. Kirchberger writes in *The First World War: An Eyewitness History,* "depended on control of the Mediterranean for communication with their African colonies."[1] To the Allies' frustration, however, the Italian government in Rome, worried about its army's level of preparedness and the conflict's unpopularity among Italians, remained stubbornly neutral.

To lure Rome into their camp, the Allies were prepared, by the spring of 1915, to promise the Italian government an array of generous financial and territorial concessions. They laid out these valuable offerings in a secret document that would come to be known as the Treaty of London. According to the covert agreement, if Italy entered the war on the Allied side within one month, Rome would receive a portion of any reparations collected from the Central Powers, substantial loans to help cover its war-related expenses, and most appealing of all to the nationalistic Italian leaders—new territory. Among the document's rich banquet of land offerings were several Austro-Hungarian possessions Rome had coveted ever since the formation of a unified Italian kingdom in 1861. These included the Italian-speaking Trentino and German-speaking South Tyrol regions to Italy's north and the port of Trieste, the Istrian Peninsula, and a slice of the predominantly Slavic Dalmatian Coast on the Adriatic Sea.

On April 26, 1915, won over by the Allies' lavish promises, Italian diplomats signed the Treaty of London along with representatives from the British, Russian, and French governments.

A World War I-era British tank breaks through a barbed wire obstacle. The First World War was the first mechanized war and featured the widespread use of chemical and biological weapons, tanks, machine guns, and airplanes.

In accordance with the pact's secret terms, Italy officially entered the conflict by declaring war on its neighbor, Austria-Hungary, a little less than a month later. When the victorious Allies gathered in Paris to hammer out a peace settlement four years after the signing of the Treaty of London, the agreement's territorial provisions would generate a great deal of bad feelings among the conference delegates. But in the spring of 1915, the Allies, relieved to have Italy in their camp, were not inclined to worry about the possible ramifications of handing out territory that was not theirs to give.

AMERICA GOES IN

Despite the Allies' satisfaction at reeling in Italy, in the wartime competition for support, "the great prize . . . was the United States," historian Alan Sharp observes.[2] For the first two and a half years of the conflict, the administration of President Woodrow Wilson stayed resolutely neutral, although sympathetic toward the Allies and particularly Britain, with which the United States shared close economic ties. In his 1796 Farewell Address, President George Washington had cautioned his fellow Americans against becoming entangled in foreign quarrels; Wilson, like virtually every U.S. president before him, took Washington's warning to heart. Thus, in May 1915, after a German U-boat (submarine) sank the *Lusitania*, a British liner carrying American passengers, Wilson simply persuaded Berlin to ban all U-boat attacks on passenger liners and neutral merchant ships rather than declare war on the Reich, as many Americans were then demanding. In early January 1917, as the Great War ground on with no end in sight, he expressed his continued determination to keep America out of the bloody conflict to his friend and adviser, Colonel Edward House. The United States was the only great world power "that is free from war today," Wilson observed to House, "and it would be a crime against civilization for us to go in."[3] Just three months later, however, on April 6, 1917, "go in" America did—and with the president's full support.

Wilson's dramatic reversal regarding U.S. involvement in World War I was rooted in two widely publicized events that took place during the winter of 1917. First, hoping to finally end the long military stalemate by cutting off vital food and munitions shipments to Great Britain, Germany resumed the policy of unrestricted submarine warfare that Wilson had pressured the Reich into abandoning in May 1915. Although German leaders realized that the renewed attacks on all vessels in British waters—neutral merchant ships as well as battleships—were bound to anger Britain's chief trading partner, the United States, and might even bring it into the conflict, they were willing to take that chance. The second event that pushed Wilson toward war was the interception and decoding by the British of the infamous Zimmermann Note from German

Foreign Secretary Arthur Zimmermann to his ambassador in Mexico. In the controversial message, Zimmermann instructed his ambassador to incite a war between Mexico and the United States to keep the Americans tied up on their side of the Atlantic and out of European affairs.

In response to Berlin resuming unrestricted submarine warfare, Wilson immediately severed diplomatic relations with the Reich. After the interception of the Zimmermann Note, and the potential threat to American national security that the secret scheme posed, the president reluctantly decided to ask Congress for a declaration of war. At a special joint session of Congress on April 2, Wilson proclaimed that, by helping to defeat the "autocratic" German Reich, American soldiers would also be helping to make "the world . . . safe for democracy."[4] With popular opinion in the country behind the president, Congress overwhelmingly voted four days later in favor of war.

A REVOLUTION IN RUSSIA AND SOME EMBARRASSING DISCLOSURES

Events in Russia made the U.S. entrance into the war even more vital to the Allies' cause. By the beginning of 1917, the imperial government's inept handling of the war had created enormous resentment among the Russian people. The inadequately equipped Russian army had suffered one loss after another to the better-armed Germans, and casualty rates among the demoralized troops had soared. Russia's civilian population was also forced to endure severe food and fuel shortages, caused by war-related economic disruptions and rampant government corruption. In March 1917, following a series of violent riots and strikes in the capital, Petrograd (formerly St. Petersburg), Czar Nicholas II was forced to step down in favor of a new provisional government appointed by Russia's elective assembly.

The leaders of the provisional government vowed to keep fighting, even as disillusionment among soldiers on the front and hungry peasants and workers at home continued to grow. In October 1917, the Bolsheviks—a radical socialist group with the irresistible slogan of "peace, land, and bread"—overthrew the provisional government in a nearly bloodless coup. To the Allies' dismay, the new regime made good on its promise of immediate peace by signing an armistice with Germany within days of taking power. The truce effectively closed the Eastern Front.

In early December, the Bolsheviks, who disdained the leaders of all the warring nations as greedy imperialists, dealt a further blow to the Allied cause when they published the secret wartime agreements among czarist Russia, France, Great Britain, and Italy. To the embarrassment of the Allies, many of the pacts' territorial provisions cast their governments in a decidedly unflattering light. The Treaty of London guaranteed Italy large tracts of Austrian territory, including areas inhabited primarily by Slavs and other non-Italians, in the event of an Allied victory. Other Allied agreements allotted most of the ethnically Polish regions under German or Austrian rule to Russia, the left bank of the Rhine River to France, and the Reich's African colonies to Britain. Allied leaders worried that the publication of these covert land deals would have a demoralizing effect on Europe's war-weary population, as well as the Americans. The war that President Wilson had portrayed in April as a noble struggle to make "the world safe . . . for democracy" was in danger of appearing as nothing more than what the Bolsheviks accused it of being: a greedy scramble for spoils.

WILSON'S FOURTEEN POINTS

In early January 1918, following the publication of these secret treaties, Wilson went before a special joint session of Congress to lay out what he saw as the Allies' chief objectives in the war, and even more importantly, for the peace to follow. Dubbed the "Fourteen Points Speech" for the number of headings under which Wilson itemized his plan for a just and lasting peace, the address would become one of the most famous

President Woodrow Wilson delivers his Fourteen Points speech before a joint session of Congress on January 8, 1918, almost a year before the armistice. His speech would serve as a basis for the terms of the German surrender at the Paris Peace Conference in 1919.

speeches ever delivered by a U.S. president. Wilson believed that the United States in his view—the most democratic and morally advanced nation on the globe—had a sacred duty to reform international politics. Through his peace plan, Wilson hoped to ensure that the secret deals, entangling military alliances, and disregard for the rights of less powerful ethnic groups would finally come to an end.

(continues on page 34)

EXCERPTS FROM WOODROW WILSON'S FOURTEEN POINTS

On January 8, 1918, nine months after the United States entered World War I, President Woodrow Wilson announced his 14-point blueprint for peace before a special joint session of Congress. Wilson hoped that his program would bring a new sense of moral direction to the Allied cause and set the terms for a just peace. The following is an excerpt from Wilson's speech:

> We entered this war because violations of right had occurred which touched us to the quick and made the life of our own people impossible unless they were corrected and the world secure once for all against their recurrence. What we demand in this war, therefore, is nothing peculiar to ourselves. It is that the world be made fit and safe to live in; and particularly that it be made safe for every peace-loving nation which, like our own, wishes to live its own life, determine its own institutions, be assured of justice and fair dealing by the other peoples of the world as against force and selfish aggression. All the peoples of the world are in effect partners in this interest, and for our own part we see very clearly that unless justice be done to others it will not be done to us. The program of the world's peace, therefore, is our program; and that program, the only possible program, as we see it, is this:
>
> I. Open covenants of peace, openly arrived at, after which there shall be no private international understandings of any kind. . . .
> II. Absolute freedom of navigation upon the seas, outside territorial waters, alike in peace and in war. . . .
> III. The removal, so far as possible, of all economic barriers . . .

IV. Adequate guarantees given and taken that national armaments will be reduced to the lowest point consistent with
domestic safety.

V. A free, open-minded, and absolutely impartial adjustment
of all colonial claims, based upon a strict observance of the
principle that in determining all such questions of sovereignty the interests of the populations concerned must have
equal weight with the equitable claims of the government
whose title is to be determined.

VI. The evacuation of all Russian territory and . . . a settlement
of all questions affecting Russia . . .

VII. Belgium . . . must be evacuated and restored. . . .

VIII. All French territory should be freed and the invaded portions
restored, and the wrong done to France by Prussia in 1871 in
the matter of Alsace-Lorraine, which has unsettled the peace
of the world for nearly fifty years, should be righted. . . .

IX. A readjustment of the frontiers of Italy should be effected
along clearly recognizable lines of nationality.

X. The peoples of Austria-Hungary, whose place among the nations we wish to see safeguarded and assured, should be accorded the freest opportunity to autonomous development.

XI. Romania, Serbia, and Montenegro should be evacuated; occupied territories restored; Serbia accorded free and secure
access to the sea; and . . . international guarantees of the
political and economic independence and territorial integrity of the several Balkan states should be entered into.

XII. The Turkish portion of the present Ottoman Empire should
be assured a secure sovereignty, but the other nationalities
which are now under Turkish rule should be assured an . . .
opportunity of autonomous development, and the Dardanelles
should be permanently opened as a free passage to the ships
and commerce of all nations under international guarantees.

XIII. An independent Polish state should be erected which should
include the territories inhabited by indisputably Polish

(continues)

(continued)

populations, which should be assured a free and secure access to the sea, and whose political and economic independence and territorial integrity should be guaranteed by international covenant.

XIV. A general association of nations must be formed under specific covenants for the purpose of affording mutual guarantees of political independence and territorial integrity to great and small states alike.*

---

*"President Woodrow Wilson's 14 Points (1918)." Our Documents Web site, http://www.ourdocuments.gov/doc.php?doc=62.

(continued from page 31)

As Charles Mee notes in *The End of Order: Versailles 1919*, Wilson made it clear in his carefully prepared address that, as far as the United States was concerned, the Great War "was being fought not simply to defeat Germany, but to defeat the very causes of war."[5] To that end, the first five points of his blueprint for peace focused on broad principles he believed must be adopted by every nation in the world: open diplomacy, unrestricted trade, absolute freedom of the seas, arms control, and an end to colonialism. The next eight points of the plan focused on specific territorial issues, including the return of Alsace-Lorraine to France, the establishment of an independent Poland with access to the sea, and the division of the autocratic, multi-ethnic Austro-Hungarian and Ottoman Empires into a number of smaller, sovereign nations. Wilson's final point was also the one that was closest to his heart: the creation of a universal association of nations to help safeguard world peace by "affording mutual guarantees of political independence and territorial integrity to great and small states alike."[6]

After more than three years of sacrifice and suffering, Wilson's inspiring vision of a more just and harmonious post-war world held enormous appeal for many ordinary Europeans. Wilson's French and British counterparts were decidedly less enthusiastic about the Fourteen Points, however. Loath to relinquish their right to blockade enemies, the British particularly disliked the second point demanding absolute freedom of the seas. The French, whose country had suffered extensive war-related damage at the hands of the German army, wanted the eighth point requiring Germany to evacuate all French territory to further stipulate that Berlin must pay reparations for Allied property losses. As long as the fighting continued, however, leaders in London and Paris were careful to at least pay lip service to Wilson's program. With Russia out of the picture, America's ongoing military support was vital to the Allied war effort, and British and French leaders were reluctant to say anything that might offend the president. Nonetheless, British Prime Minister David Lloyd George questioned the practicality of Wilson's plan in private, while French Premier Georges Clemenceau mockingly noted that, while "God himself was content with 10 commandments, Wilson modestly inflicted Fourteen Points on us."[7]

THE "WAR TO END ALL WARS" FINALLY DRAWS TO A CLOSE

With a regular army of just under 130,000, the United States entered the war in April 1917 woefully unprepared for battle. It would be well into 1918 before the United States would be able to send a sufficient number of trained troops to Europe to have any real impact on the fighting. By the spring of 1918, with the number of American troops on the continent steadily mounting, Berlin decided the time had to come to make a no-holds-barred bid for victory. In March, the kaiser's army launched a large-scale offensive near the Somme River in France. For the next three months, the Germans struck repeatedly at the Allied line. Then in July, the tide of the fighting turned against them at the Marne River, and the Allied forces, by now significantly bolstered by American troops, grabbed the offensive. By September, the Germans were in retreat and their allies were falling by the wayside one by one. Bulgaria accepted an Allied armistice in September, and the Ottoman Empire, after being driven out of its Middle Eastern colonies by British forces, surrendered in October. Earlier that same month, the German government, having been advised by its military leaders in the German High Command to sue for peace immediately, had quietly sent a note to President Wilson asking him to take charge of arranging a cease-fire and the peace negotiations to follow. "As the basis for its negotiations" with the other belligerents, the note said, "the German government accepts . . . the program laid down by the President of the United States," in other words, the Fourteen Points. When the Germans' "plight became unbearable," Charles Mee writes, "they turned not to the French or the English to sue for peace but to Wilson, whose speeches had promised again and again a peace of justice for all."[8]

Talks between the German government and Wilson, who turned out to be a considerably tougher negotiator than Berlin had anticipated, dragged on for weeks. Only after Germany consented to withdraw all its troops beyond the Rhine River as soon as an armistice was concluded, surrender large quantities of war materials, and institute democratic political reforms, did Wilson officially inform Britain and France of Berlin's request for a cease-fire and peace settlement. Early on the morning of November 11, 1918, in a quiet forest glen near Compiègne, France, delegates of the new German Republic, formed just two days earlier following the abdication of Kaiser Wilhelm II, officially accepted the Allied armistice terms. Just a little more than a week earlier, on November 3, the last of Germany's Central Power allies, Austria-Hungary, had also agreed to a cease-fire. The conflict optimistically dubbed the "war to end all wars" was finally over.

The Peace
Conference Begins

On Saturday, January 18, 1919, the Paris Peace Conference opened in the recently renamed "Salon of Peace" of the Quai d'Orsay, the headquarters for the French Ministry of Foreign Affairs. On that date nearly a half-century earlier, the new German Empire celebrated its victory over France in the Franco-Prussian War by crowning its first kaiser in a lavish ceremony at the Palace of Versailles, barely 10 miles (16 kilometers) away. That the Paris Peace Conference was launched on the anniversary of the Reich's founding was no coincidence. The assembly's 77-year-old chairman, Premier Georges Clemenceau, a survivor of the German siege of Paris in 1871, had chosen the date deliberately. In his opening remarks to the delegates, Clemenceau's colleague, French President Raymond Poincaré, stressed the significance of January 18, not only for

France but also for all the Allied combatants in Europe's most recent war, a war he blamed squarely on imperial Germany. Poincaré declared:

> On this day, 48 years ago, the German Empire was proclaimed by an army of invasion . . . in the Château at Versailles. It was consecrated by the theft of two French provinces [Alsace and Lorraine]. . . . Born in injustice, it has ended in opprobrium [disgrace]. You are assembled in order to repair the evil that it has done and to prevent a recurrence of it. You hold in your hands the future of the world.[1]

WHO WAS AT THE PEACE CONFERENCE— AND WHO WAS NOT

Listening to the French president's dramatic words that day were delegates from 32 nations, all of whom had declared for the Allies at some point during the conflict, though only a relative few had actually made a significant contribution to the fighting. Hailing from all corners of the globe, the peacemakers were a diverse group. Some represented great world powers like the United States, the British Empire, and Japan. Others spoke for lesser powers such as Belgium, Cuba, Siam (Thailand), and the still-emerging state of Czechoslovakia.

One great power noticeably absent from the Quai d'Orsay was Russia. Although the Russian Empire's ill-supplied and ineptly led troops seldom prevailed on the battlefield, Russia's contribution to the war effort was enormous when measured in terms of lives lost. From August 1914 until the closing of the Eastern Front in late 1917, an estimated 1.7 million Russian soldiers perished—a full 30 percent of all Allied deaths in World War I. Russia's location provided another powerful argument for including the sprawling nation in the treaty negotiations. Some of the most pressing territorial questions the treaty makers confronted in 1919 directly impacted Russia, since they concerned emerging states that had once been under czarist rule, including Latvia, Estonia, Lithuania, and Poland.

Despite the compelling reasons for including Russia in the talks, the French, British, and American officials did not invite representatives of the new Russian government to the Paris Peace Conference. Ever since the Bolsheviks overthrew the provisional government, the Allies had been watching events in Russia with growing alarm. In January 1918, the Bolsheviks had dismissed Russia's democratically elected assembly at gunpoint; in July, they executed the deposed czar and his entire family. Adding to the peacemakers' concerns was the Bolsheviks' avowed intention to spread their revolutionary Communist ideas beyond Russia's borders. The fact that Communists (including some who had been trained in Moscow) had seized power briefly in southern Germany and Hungary during the final chaotic days of the war only seemed to confirm Allied fears regarding the Bolsheviks' subversive plans for the rest of Europe.

To justify Russia's exclusion from the conference, Chairman Clemenceau argued that the Bolsheviks had forfeited their right to sit at the peace table by withdrawing from the fighting in late 1917 and negotiating a separate peace treaty with Germany a few months later. Moreover, Clemenceau and the other conference organizers contended that it was unclear whether Bolshevik leader Vladimir Lenin and his colleagues actually had the authority to speak for the Russian people: Discontent with the repressive Communist regime had escalated into a full-blown civil war in 1918, pitting the Bolsheviks or "Reds" against the "Whites," a loose coalition of monarchists, republicans, and moderate socialists. By the time the Peace Conference convened in January 1919, two leading White generals, bolstered by money and arms from the Allies, had founded what were in effect rival governments in Siberia and southern Russia. Although the Bolsheviks would eventually crush their White opponents, the outcome of Russia's bloody civil war remained in doubt during the Peace Conference.

Aside from Russia, another nation that was noticeably missing from the Salon of Peace on January 18, 1919, was Germany. Although President Wilson and Prime Minister Lloyd George had toyed with the idea of asking representatives from Germany's recently established republican government to participate in the treaty writing, Clemenceau strongly opposed the idea. The Paris Conference never officially barred the Weimar Republic—as Germany's new democratic government came to be known—from the negotiations. But as the peace talks dragged on through the winter and into the spring of 1919, it became clear that the Germans would not receive an invitation to Paris, at least not until the treaty was completed and ready for their signatures.

THE COUNCIL OF TEN

Delegates from nearly three dozen nations were invited to the Paris Conference. Yet it quickly became evident that the representatives of the chief Allied powers would be making most of the decisions. In deference to the lesser powers, the French, British, and American organizers declared that delegates from all the recognized Allied states at the assembly could attend a weekly Plenary Conference, during which treaty-related issues would be discussed in a general forum. Members of the Plenary Conference were also given the opportunity to form commissions that were entrusted with studying and making recommendations regarding various aspects of the peace settlement, such as the establishment of the international peacekeeping organization proposed in Wilson's Fourteen Points. Even before the Paris Conference officially opened, however, its powerful organizers had quietly determined that the assembly's real decision-making body was not to be the Plenary Conference but rather a considerably smaller group, the Supreme Council.

After some debate, conference planners decided that the Supreme Council, renamed the Council of Ten, would be composed of two representatives each from just five nations. Meeting entirely behind closed doors, this elite committee would include the four leading Western powers—France, Great Britain, the United States, and Italy—and one rapidly rising Eastern power—Japan, by far the most industrially and militarily advanced country in Asia in 1919. Since each of the five powers came to Paris with different and sometimes sharply conflicting conceptions of what constituted the ideal German settlement, it soon became apparent to most participants and observers that agreeing on a peace treaty would be difficult.

FRANCE'S AIMS ON THE COUNCIL OF TEN

As France's premier as well as its minister of war, Georges Clemenceau (nicknamed "The Tiger" for his legendary courage and tenacity), had held his country together through the darkest days of World War I. Yet when the fighting finally ended in November 1918, Clemenceau never doubted for a moment that his most challenging task still lay ahead. "Yes, we have won the war and not without difficulty," he remarked to an aide immediately after the German armistice was declared, "but now we are going to have to win the peace, and that will perhaps be even more difficult."[2]

Without question, no other nation represented on the Council of Ten had suffered more at the hands of the Reich or had more at stake in the German settlement than France. Approximately 1.3 million French soldiers—fully one out of four French men ages 18 to 30—perished in World War I, along with at least 400,000 French civilians. France lost a significantly higher percentage of its prewar population than any other nation in the conflict, including Russia. Moreover, since France was the war's major battleground for four long years, the country also sustained considerably more physical damage than any other nation on either side of the conflict. In those areas where

A 1924 photo of Georges Clemenceau, the French prime minister and co-formulator of the Treaty of Versailles. During the treaty negotiations, Clemenceau took a hard line with Germany and its allies.

the most intense fighting had taken place, Margaret MacMillan notes in *Paris 1919: Six Months That Changed the World*, "great stretches of land were pitted with shell holes, scarred by deep trenches, marked with row upon row of crosses."[3] Adding insult to injury, during the final days of the war, retreating German troops devastated France's most industrialized region and the source of most of its coal and iron ore, the Northeast. The Germans flooded mines, tore up railroad tracks, dynamited bridges and factories, and razed entire villages. Any just peace, Clemenceau was convinced, would require Berlin to compensate the French people for the terrible damage its armies had inflicted on their country.

Clemenceau's determination that the peace settlement impose heavy reparations on Germany was not only motivated by a desire to make Berlin pay for its crimes against the French people; he also viewed reparations as a means of weakening the country that had posed the greatest threat to French national security for five decades. Twice in the last 50 years, German troops had invaded France: in 1870 during the Franco-Prussian War and again in August 1914. In light of France's past experiences, Clemenceau was anxious to ensure that Germany would never again be strong enough to overrun his homeland. Consequently, he came to the negotiations in January 1919 resolved to seek peace terms so stringent that Germany would be weakened economically, militarily, and territorially. For Clemenceau, the ideal peace settlement would not only dismantle Germany's navy—which had been partially achieved under the armistice's terms—but also drastically reduce the size of its army. Furthermore, it would significantly shrink Germany's size, preferably by forcing it to relinquish all of the Rhineland, the part of Germany that lies to the west of the Rhine River. Lastly, in addition to restoring the French provinces of Alsace and Lorraine, Clemenceau wanted the peacemakers to give France western Germany's iron ore and coal-rich Saar Valley, to compensate for the hundreds of French mines and factories destroyed during the war and to permanently weaken Germany's highly industrialized economy.

THE VARYING PEACE GOALS OF GREAT BRITAIN, ITALY, AND JAPAN

In common with Clemenceau, the chief British negotiator on the Council of Ten, Prime Minister Lloyd George, also hoped to reduce Germany's military capabilities, particularly at sea, since the Reich had been Britain's main naval rival before the war. In the recent British parliamentary election, Lloyd George's party had been reelected by a landslide with the slogan "squeeze the German lemon 'til the pips [seeds] squeak."[4] In truth, however, while he wanted Britain to have a share of any German reparation payments, the prime minister wanted Germany to remain a viable economic power, both for its value to Britain as a trading partner and as a buffer against Bolshevik Russia and France. He believed that maintaining a strict balance of power on the continent in which no single nation—be it France or Russia or Germany—was able to dominate was in the best interests of peace and British national security.

Solidifying his nation's claim to the Austro-Hungarian territories promised it by the Treaty of London of 1915 was the major aim of Italy's chief representative on the Council of Ten, Prime Minister Vittorio Orlando. Orlando never doubted that Italy deserved the spoils of war outlined in the secret Allied agreement as compensation for the country's economic and human losses during the conflict. His French, British, and American colleagues on the council, however, were far less impressed by the Italian war effort than Orlando: Lloyd George and Clemenceau in particular "thought the Italians had not fought with much enthusiasm," Charles Mee maintains.[5] Moreover, by January 1919, much of the new territory that Orlando sought was no longer under Austrian or Hungarian control, including the Dalmatian coast and the Adriatic port of Fiume (today Rijeka, Croatia). Rather, it had become part

A scene during the peace conference held at Versailles in 1919. The long negotiations between the victorious Allies were intense and often fractious.

of the emerging nation of Yugoslavia, originally known as the Kingdom of Serbs, Croats, and Slovenes. Since the Serbs, who comprised most of the new kingdom's population, had fought valiantly with the Allies, French, British, and American peacemakers were extremely reluctant to accommodate Italy's wishes regarding Fiume and the other predominantly Slavic areas that the Yugoslavs thought of as their own.

Like Orlando, the Japanese members of the Council of Ten, Sutemi Chinda and Keishiro Matsui, Tokyo's ambassadors to Great Britain and France, respectively, were mainly concerned with solidifying their nation's territorial claims.

Most importantly, the Japanese government wanted the Peace Conference to confirm its takeover of German territorial and economic rights in the northern Chinese province of Shantung

THE MANDATE SYSTEM AND WILSON'S COMMITMENT TO JUSTICE AND HUMAN RIGHTS

Aside from drafting a constitution for the League of Nations, the Peace Conference's only other significant accomplishment during its first month in session was the creation of a mandate system to administer the former colonies of Germany and Turkey until they were judged ready for independence. From the beginning, the chief promoter of the mandate system at the Paris Conference was Woodrow Wilson. His compatriots at the conference with occupying armies in former Central Power colonies simply wanted to annex the territories their troops had wrested from the enemy. To Wilson, however, outright annexation constituted a clear violation of the fundamental principles of justice and human rights that he believed must underpin any truly equitable and lasting peace settlement. Hundreds of thousands of people lived in the onetime colonies of Germany and Turkey. These native populations, Wilson maintained, deserved the right of self-determination, rather than merely being handed over to a new set of foreign rulers. "Peoples and provinces are not to be bartered about from sovereignty to sovereignty as if they were mere chattels and pawns in a game," he insisted.*

According to the mandate system, the League of Nations had the authority to place former imperial territories under the supervision of an established power. With the League of Nations providing general oversight, the established power

(Shandong), which Japanese troops had occupied since expelling the Germans in 1914. Japan had only taken a peripheral role in the fighting during World War I and sustained the

would act as a disinterested trustee over the region, promoting the welfare of its inhabitants in a variety of ways, including protecting them from stronger countries and performing humanitarian work. At the same time, it would help to prepare the former colonists economically, politically, and militarily for full independence, a process that could take a few months or many years.

The mandate plan had prejudicial overtones in its assumption that the colonies' indigenous populations could not be entrusted with self-rule without first being tutored by one of the more politically and economically "advanced" powers. Yet to Wilson, this system of international trusteeship represented a far more just way of acting than the old colonial methods of annexation and economic exploitation. Even so, the president was clearly concerned about how the mandate system might strike others, worrying that cynics might dismiss it as no more than a convenient excuse for the Allies to hold onto the overseas territories they had seized during the war. This is evident in Wilson's insistence that the Council of Ten not begin distributing mandates for the former colonies at once among the victors but rather wait until after the final covenant for the League of Nations had been drawn up and approved. Otherwise, Wilson asserted, some might charge "that the Great Powers first portioned out the helpless parts of the world, and then formed a League of Nations."**

---

*Alan Sharp, *The Versailles Settlement: Peacemaking in Paris, 1919.* New York: St. Martin's Press, 1991, p. 15.

**Ibid., p. 162.

least casualties and material loss of any nation on the Council of Ten. Nonetheless, since the British had secretly agreed to Japan's takeover of Shantung in return for its naval assistance in the Mediterranean in 1917, Chinda and Matsui were hopeful that the Council of Ten would validate their nation's claim on the province, even in the face of strong protests from China.

WILSON'S LEAGUE OF NATIONS

The most important goal of America's chief negotiator on the Council of Ten, President Wilson, was the establishment of an international peacekeeping organization, or League of Nations. By mediating any future disputes between nations, Wilson optimistically believed, the league would bring an end to all war. Wilson was also hopeful that the League of Nations would provide a body to which any flaws within the peace treaties with Germany and the other Central Powers could be taken for deliberation and adjustment. In Wilson's view, MacMillan notes, "If [the League] could be brought into being, then everything else would sooner or later fall into place. If the peace terms were imperfect, there would be plenty of time later for the League to correct them. Many new borders had to be drawn; if they were not quite right, the League would sort them out."[6]

Although Chairman Clemenceau had wanted to work out the details of the German settlement immediately, Wilson urged that the first order of business at the Paris Conference be the drafting of a covenant (constitution) for the League of Nations. Wilson had little trouble convincing his colleagues, even Clemenceau, to go along with his request. After four long and agonizing years of war, the president's proposal for an international peacekeeping organization was extremely popular among European leaders and their citizens. Consequently, none of the elected officials serving on the council wanted to give the impression that they were hindering Wilson's beloved project in any way.

Woodrow Wilson photographed at the Quai d'Orsay at the start of the Paris Peace Conference. During the treaty negotiations, Wilson was determined to establish the League of Nations, which he believed would help keep the postwar peace.

On January 25, just a week after the official opening of the Peace Conference, the Plenary Conference officially approved the creation of a commission on the League of Nations to be headed by Wilson. Fourteen countries would eventually be represented on the commission, with the five major powers on the Council of Ten awarded two delegates each and the remaining nine countries one delegate each. Despite its size, under the president's efficient if sometimes authoritarian management, the league commission "worked with a speed and determination that was unique at this stage of the Paris Negotiations," Alan Sharp observes.[7] "Wilson, in the chair, was brisk," MacMillan writes, "discouraging speeches and discussions of details and pushing the League in the direction he wanted."[8]

THE COVENANT OF THE LEAGUE OF NATIONS

Most commission members—either because they saw little fault in Wilson's vision of the league's basic purpose, procedures, and organizational structure, or because they found the American president intimidating—deferred to his leadership. The only significant objections came from the two French delegates. Egged on by Clemenceau, they fought stubbornly to give the League of Nations its own standing army over the strong objections of Wilson and the two British delegates. Understandably shaken by the fact that their country had suffered two major invasions in the last 50 years, Clemenceau and his commission colleagues worried that, without a permanent fighting force of its own, the league would have little power against potential aggressors. Merely threatening aggressive nations with economic sanctions, as Wilson and the British proposed, was not enough, the French maintained. Wilson accused the French delegates of trying to make the League of Nations into an old-fashioned military alliance, no different from the ones that had helped drag Europe into World War I in the first place. Far from being a military coalition, Wilson insisted, the league had to be a forum in which disputes between nations could be resolved peacefully *before* the contending parties resorted to military alliances.

By February 13, with Wilson still refusing to give an inch, the French ended their campaign for a league army. The next day the commission presented a preliminary plan for the covenant to the Plenary Conference for review. The 26-article covenant called for a general assembly composed of all league members; an Executive Council with five permanent members (the United States, Great Britain, France, Italy, and Japan) plus four nonpermanent members "to be selected by the Assembly from time to time in its discretion"; and an administrative arm to carry out the League of Nations' decisions. In what would become the best-known provision of the covenant, the tenth or so-called collective security article, member states had to pledge to "respect and preserve as against external aggression the territorial integrity and existing political independence of all Members of the League." Other articles required members to bring any disputes between their countries and other nations before the Executive Council for study and proposed resolution and stipulated that, if the council's decision on the disagreement was not unanimous, states had the right to "take such action as they shall consider necessary for the maintenance of right and justice."[9] According to Article 16, these individual actions could include military sanctions, but the league itself was prohibited from imposing any punishment stronger than economic sanctions against aggressors.

Today, most scholars agree that the covenant submitted by Wilson's commission to the Plenary Conference on February 14, 1919, had a number of serious weaknesses, most notably its requirement that all council decisions on the handling of international disputes be unanimous. The document would undergo a few minor revisions before its final acceptance by the Plenary Conference on April 28. To Wilson's delight, in addition to approving the covenant that day, the conference also agreed to his request that its 26 articles be included in the main bodies of all the treaties with the defeated Central Powers. It was a moment of personal triumph for Wilson in what had otherwise proven to be a frustrating two and a half months since the preliminary covenant was completed. The president had secured his cherished League of Nations. Yet, as the great powers got down to hammering out the specific provisions of the German settlement in March and April 1919, it became evident that the rest of his idealistic 14-point peace program would be considerably harder to attain.

Forging a German Settlement

In mid-February 1919, after the Paris Peace Conference had been in session for a month, Woodrow Wilson and David Lloyd George took hiatuses from their treaty-writing duties to tend to political business at home. Shortly after the two left France, an anarchist fired several shots at Georges Clemenceau as he was stepping into his car on February 19. One bullet struck the 77-year-old premier in the chest, narrowly missing his heart and lungs. In mid-March, when Wilson and Lloyd George finally returned to the conference, they found the remarkably resilient "Tiger of France" already back at work and eager to begin to shape the final provisions of the German treaty. With spring almost upon them, and many of the most complex issues concerning the peace terms still unresolved, Wilson and Lloyd George felt pressured to pick up the pace of the negotiations. With this in mind, Wilson, Lloyd George, and Clemenceau resolved to streamline the conference's chief decision-making mechanism, the Council of Ten, by dismissing every other member except the three of them and Italian Prime Minister Vittorio Orlando.

THE TREATY'S MILITARY PROVISIONS

One of the first issues tackled by the new "Council of Four" was the question of what military terms to set with Germany. Determined to prevent Germany from waging another war, all the council members wanted the treaty to include stringent military conditions. In the end, they would leave Germany "with something closer to a police force than an army," Margaret MacMillan notes.[1] According to the military provisions formulated by the council, German conscription was to be abolished and the army reduced to just 100,000 men. Germany's severely depleted fighting force was expressly forbidden the use of military aircraft, heavy artillery, tanks, or poison gas—weapons used by both sides in the war. Only a handful of German factories were authorized to manufacture arms, munitions, and other war materials, and the import of all war materials from other countries was banned. Any existing stores of weapons were to be immediately destroyed.

The Council of Four also agreed that Germany's navy should be strictly limited to just 15,000 men, no submarines, and a skeleton surface fleet. Under the terms of the 1918 armistice, the existing German surface fleet along with their crews had been interned at Scapa Flow in the Orkneys, a remote island group off the coast of Scotland. The question of what to do with the fleet's 74 state-of-the-art battleships, cruisers, and destroyers was hotly debated among the Big Four. Lloyd George, the representative of the greatest naval power at the Paris Conference, wanted to sink all of the ships. Eager to build up their own countries' considerably smaller fleets, Clemenceau

Workers dismantle a German tank circa 1920. According to the Treaty of Versailles, Germany's armed forces were to be strictly limited and its army was not allowed to have tanks, among other armaments.

and Orlando wanted the vessels to be distributed among the major Allied countries. In June, "when it had become clear that, whatever was decided, the ships would not be allowed to return to Germany," Ruth Henig writes, the vessels' defiant crews "finally resolved the issue" for the Allies by sinking the entire German fleet themselves.[2]

Although the European Allies devised the stringent military clauses, the influence of Wilson, whose Fourteen Points called for the voluntary "reduction of all national armaments to the lowest point consistent with domestic safety," is evident in the preamble to the treaty's military section.[3] Germany was being deprived of most of its weaponry, the preamble declared, "in order to render possible the initiation of a general limitation of the armaments of all nations."[4] That the voluntary international disarmament that the treaty optimistically claimed would follow in the wake of German disarmament never, in fact, occurred would prove a source of resentment among Germans for many years to come.

THE CONTROVERSY OVER REPARATIONS: "MAKING GERMANY PAY"

Throughout the spring of 1919, the financial settlement with Germany remained a source of contention within the Council of Four. Since they were convinced that Berlin was to blame for starting the war, all the members thought Germany should pay some compensation to those Allied nations whose civilian populations had suffered the most. Clearly, the French and the Belgians, within whose borders the bulk of the fighting had occurred, deserved something for their substantial losses. Yet Lloyd George, who had repeatedly promised the British people that he would make the German aggressors pay, was determined that his nation should receive a sizable share of the reparations money as well. To that end, Lloyd George wanted the Germans to pay higher indemnities than even Clemenceau had sought. He demanded that Germany be held responsible not only for the damage its troops had caused to civilian property but also for pensions and allowances for wounded Allied veterans and the widows and orphans of deceased servicemen. According to historian Alan Sharp, Lloyd George sought to include military pensions and allowances in the financial settlement because he realized that, if Germany paid only for damages to civilian property, France and Belgium would receive the lion's share of the reparations and Britain would get virtually nothing—even though the British government had

German sailors in a boat approaching the shore after they destroyed their ship, the *Nurnberg*. On June 21, 1919, the German navy's commander, Rear Admiral Ludwig von Reuter, gave orders to scuttle the fleet so the ships would not fall into Allied hands.

spent more money fighting the Reich and its allies than either the Belgian or French governments had.

Not surprisingly, Clemenceau—determined to weaken Germany in every way possible—enthusiastically supported Lloyd George's proposal. Wilson, however, was incensed by the idea of making Germany responsible for Allied pensions as well as civilian damages. Adding soldiers' pensions and allowances to Germany's reparations bill, Wilson realized, would significantly inflate its financial obligations to the Allies. Saddling Germany with a large debt was not only immoral, he believed, but also unwise. He feared leaving Germany economically weak would just encourage the ambitions of its neighbor,

Russia, whose Bolshevik leaders had repeatedly proclaimed their desire to export Communism to the rest of Europe. By early April, however, the president—who would suffer a massive stroke just six months later—was in failing health. Under pressure from Clemenceau and Lloyd George and "on the verge of physical exhaustion," his biographer, Thomas Knock, writes, "Wilson capitulated on April 5."[5] Unable to agree on either an exact amount for the reparations or the varying percentages of the payments that France, Belgium, Great Britain, Italy, and other Allied claimants should receive, the Big Four appointed a special Reparations Commission to make a final determination. Composed of representatives from the leading Allied powers, plus Belgium and Yugoslavia, the commission was given two years, until May 1, 1921, to study and deliberate on the reparations problem. Until the commission came up with a final amount, the council agreed that Germany should make immediate reparations to the Allies in the amount of 20 billion gold marks.

In an effort to justify this and the larger claim the Reparations Commission would make on Germany in the future, the Council of Four approved what became one of the most controversial provisions of the peace settlement: the so-called war-guilt clause. According to the clause—Article 231 of the completed Treaty of Versailles—the war had been forced upon the Allies by German "aggression" and consequently Germany must assume full responsibility "for causing all the damage to which the Allied . . . Governments and their nationals have been subjected."[6] Although the article was an honest reflection of the treaty-writers' beliefs, including such a clause in the peace settlement was undiplomatic, to say the least. "This clause," historian Henig observes, "was to cause lasting resentment in Germany" that would soon be exploited with enormous success by an embittered and ruthlessly ambitious World War I veteran named Adolf Hitler.[7]

THE FIGHT OVER GERMANY'S WESTERN FRONTIER

While the Big Four were trying to finalize an agreement on reparations, they were also engaged in a heated debate over Germany's western frontier. Clemenceau demanded that Germany's western boundary be moved as far back as the Rhine River to protect France against a future German invasion. The Rhineland—the part of Germany that lies to the west of the Rhine River and stretches northward from Alsace-Lorraine to the Netherlands—could become an independent state, Clemenceau proposed. Or all of it could be independent except one small but valuable area known as the Saar, which Clemenceau argued should be awarded to France. Located on the northern tip of Alsace-Lorraine, the Saar possessed extensive coal and iron ore deposits. Considering that retreating German troops destroyed hundreds of French mines and factories in 1918, Clemenceau believed that France needed and deserved control over the Saar and its abundant mineral resources.

Wilson and Lloyd George adamantly opposed Clemenceau's demands. Although the two leaders were sympathetic to France's demand for German coal to compensate for the deliberate flooding of its mines by the kaiser's troops, they saw no reason why France should be given control over the entire Saar. Moreover, forcing the Saar's German inhabitants to live under French rule ran counter to what Wilson had championed in his Fourteen Points and believed was critical to a lasting and just peace—the right of a people to decide its own political destiny. Since the vast majority of Rhinelanders wished to remain within Germany, Wilson rejected Clemenceau's scheme for an independent Rhineland. Lloyd George objected for more practical reasons: ripping the Rhineland away from Germany, he feared, would merely sow the seeds for a future war.

For a time it seemed that the dispute over the future of the Rhineland might break up the Peace Conference. On March 28, after a particularly heated discussion between the French premier and the American president regarding Germany's western boundaries, Clemenceau denounced Wilson as "the friend of Germany" and stormed out of the meeting.[8] A week later, with Clemenceau still refusing to give an inch regarding French annexation of the Saar, Wilson ordered the captain of the ship that had brought him to Europe to prepare to convey him back to the United States. "I have been doing a lot of thinking, thinking what would be the outcome on the world if these French politicians were . . . allowed to have their way and secure all that they claim France is entitled to," he confided to his personal physician, Cary Grayson. "My opinion is that if they had their way, the world would go to pieces in a very short while."[9]

Shaken by Wilson's threat to abandon the Peace Conference altogether, Clemenceau finally expressed his willingness to compromise on the Saar and the rest of the Rhineland. In return for French ownership of the Saar coal mines, Clemenceau agreed to relinquish his annexation plan. In return, Wilson and Lloyd George agreed that, instead of handing over the Saar to Germany immediately, a special League of Nations commission would administer the area for 15 years. At the end of this period, the Saar's inhabitants could decide in a plebiscite (a region-wide vote by the electorate on an important issue) whether they wanted to continue under the direction of the League of Nations, rejoin Germany, or become part of France. In 1935, when the plebiscite was held, the people of the Saar voted overwhelmingly for inclusion in Germany.

Soon after the Saar compromise, the Council of Four also reached an agreement regarding Germany's western frontier: Germany would return Alsace-Lorraine to France and cede the small border districts of Eupen and Malmédy to Belgium, but it could retain possession of the Rhineland. In return for Clemenceau's willingness to abandon his independent Rhineland plan, Wilson and Lloyd George agreed to the permanent demilitarization of the entire left bank of the Rhine. German military forces and installations would be forbidden on the right or eastern bank of the Rhine to a distance of 31

According to the Allied peacemakers, plebiscites would decide the fate of disputed regions in Europe. Here, Germans are on their way to a polling station on July 11, 1920, to vote in the plebiscite for East Prussia, part of the German Republic.

miles (50 kilometers). The two leaders also reluctantly gave in to Clemenceau's demands for an inter-Allied occupation of the Rhineland and of the three strategic bridgeheads (fortifications commanding the end of a bridge nearest the enemy) of Cologne, Coblenz, and Mainz for 15 years. The Allied occupation was to be divided into three zones, with the first evacuated after five years, the second after 10 years, and the third after 15 years, assuming the Germans had met all of their reparation obligations by that time. Clemenceau managed to wring one more concession out of Wilson and Lloyd George in return for keeping the Rhineland German: a treaty guaranteeing Anglo-American military assistance to France in case of a future

German attack. Parliament ratified the Anglo-American Treaty of Guarantee in the summer of 1919, but with the stipulation that it would not go into effect until the U.S. Congress approved the equivalent treaty with France. Congress, however, never approved the Treaty of Guarantee, leaving France without any assurances of assistance in the event of another invasion by its more populous neighbor to the east.

SETTING GERMANY'S NORTHERN AND EASTERN BORDERS

While Wilson, Clemenceau, and Lloyd George were struggling to agree on Germany's western boundaries, they were also trying to set its eastern and northern frontiers. Denmark, Germany's neighbor to the northwest, wanted the mostly Danish-speaking northern section of the duchy of Schleswig, which had been conquered by Prussia shortly before German unification. Guided by the principle of self-determination, the council concurred that the people of northern and central Schleswig be given the right to a plebiscite to decide whether they should join Denmark or reunite with Germany. When the plebiscites were held early in 1920, Schleswig's northern zone voted to join Denmark and its German-speaking central zone opted to stay with southern Schleswig and Germany. (The German-Danish border established by the 1920 plebiscite remains unchanged today.)

While in the north "Germany's borders were settled relatively easily," notes historian MacMillan, drawing the German Republic's borders with its new neighbor to the east, Poland, proved to be a lengthy and contentious process for the Council of Four.[10] Poland had been independent until the late 1700s, when its predatory neighbors, Russia, Prussia, and Austria, carved the nation up among them. A power vacuum in Eastern Europe, which Polish nationalists were quick to exploit, was created with the Bolshevik Revolution of 1917 and Russia's subsequent withdrawal from the war; the collapse of the Austro-Hungarian Empire during the final months of the fighting; and, finally, the surrender of Germany in November 1918. When the Paris Peace Conference opened, Poland's status as an independent state was already established even if its precise borders were not. In his Fourteen Points, Wilson had called for a reconstituted Poland to "include territories inhabited by indisputably Polish populations, which should be assured a free and secure access to the sea."[11] Yet, as the president would soon discover, ensuring both an economic outlet to the Baltic Sea for the Poles and creating a Polish state whose population was "indisputably" Polish in its ethnic makeup, was simply infeasible.

For Poland to have a free and secure "corridor" to the Baltic Sea, Polish leaders insisted that the Council of Four award their state a wide swath of two eastern German provinces: West Prussia and Posen. If Poland were allotted the portions of Posen and West Prussia it wanted along with the Baltic seaport of Danzig (now Gdańsk), at least 2 million citizens, mostly of German descent, would be incorporated into the new Polish state. This clearly violated the principle of self-determination Wilson had touted as a key component of any just and enduring peace. Nonetheless, convinced that a strong Poland was vital to the future stability of Europe, Wilson, along with Clemenceau, supported Polish demands for Danzig and a wide corridor of land to the Baltic through Posen and West Prussia. Because of its strategic location between Bolshevik Russia and Germany, Wilson and Clemenceau believed that Poland could serve as a critical barrier to Communism's westward spread. Lloyd George, although also deeply concerned about the expansion of Communism beyond Russia's borders, saw the situation differently from his French and American colleagues. He feared that forcing large numbers of Germans to live under Polish rule could result in a nationalist backlash so powerful that it might even push a resentful Germany toward the Bolsheviks. "The greatest danger that I see in the present situation is that

Germany may throw in her lot with Bolshevism and place her resources, her brains, her vast organizing power at the disposal of the revolutionary fanatics whose dream it is to conquer the world for Bolshevism by force of arms," Lloyd George warned his colleagues.[12]

After weeks of squabbling over Germany's eastern frontiers, the Council of Four finally reached a compromise on the so-called Polish Corridor and the port of Danzig. Rather than give Danzig, with its overwhelmingly German population, to Poland, it was declared, at Lloyd George's suggestion, a "free city," under the supervision of the League of Nations but tied to Poland economically. Lloyd George also persuaded the council to allow two districts along the borders of the Polish Corridor with large German majorities, Allenstein and Marienwerder, to hold plebiscites to determine their fate. In March 1920, both districts voted decisively to stay within Germany. Aside from the Polish Corridor territory, the council decided to give Upper Silesia, another ethnically mixed region along the German-Polish frontier, to Poland. Located in the far southeastern corner of Germany, Upper Silesia was claimed by Poland's new leaders as "indisputably Polish," even though it had not been under Polish rule since the fourteenth century. Although small in size, the area had rich mineral resources. Before the war, Henig writes, "it had provided Germany with 23 percent of her coal, 80 percent of her zinc and a large part of her iron."[13]

ITALY AND JAPAN MAKE DEMANDS

Until April, when the Council of Four tackled the issue of Italy's borders in the Adriatic region, Prime Minister Orlando's participation in the council's discussions had been extremely limited. His overriding concern at the Peace Conference had been securing the territory for Italy promised by France, Great Britain, and Russia in the Treaty of London of 1915, most notably Trentino and South Tyrol in the north and the Istrian Peninsula, the port of Trieste, and part of Dalmatia on the Adriatic Sea. To that list, Orlando had also added the predominantly Slavic city of Fiume at the head of the Adriatic, which the Treaty of London had assigned to Croatia, now part of the emerging nation of Yugoslavia. Bending to pressure from his Allied colleagues, Wilson had agreed early in the conference that Italy should receive the South Tyrol and Trentino—even though giving the largely German-speaking South Tyrol to Italy violated the ninth of his Fourteen Points, which stated that Italy's postwar frontiers should be drawn along "clearly recognizable lines of nationality."[14] When it came to Italy's eastern frontiers with Yugoslavia, however, Wilson was far more hesitant to discard the principle of ethnic and national self-determination.

By late April, Wilson had reluctantly agreed that Italy rather than Yugoslavia should have the Adriatic port of Trieste and parts of the predominantly Slavic areas of Istria and Dalmatia. Yet he adamantly refused to give Fiume to Italy, causing Orlando to storm out of the Peace Conference on April 21. Not until 1920 would the question of Fiume's future be resolved, after Italian, Allied, and Yugoslav negotiators agreed that the port should be declared a free city. Fiume lost its independent status just four years later when Italy's fascist leader, Benito Mussolini, bullied the Yugoslav government into accepting Italian control of the city.

On April 26, less than a week after Orlando walked out of the Paris Conference over Fiume, the Japanese delegation threatened to do likewise over China's Shantung Province, which Japan had been occupying since 1914 when its troops wrested the mineral-rich peninsula from German control. Japan's demand to remain in Shantung despite strong Chinese protests clearly conflicted with the principle of self-determination. Nonetheless, despite his firm stance on Fiume, Wilson reluctantly agreed to turn over Shantung to Japan with the stipulation that the Japanese government would restore Chinese sovereignty on the peninsula within five years "through the mediation of the League of Nations."[15] Although sympathetic to China, Wilson worried that, if he crossed the Japanese on Shantung, they would retaliate by refusing to join the League of Nations. Already worried that the Italians might withdraw from the peacekeeping organization over the Fiume dispute, Wilson did not want to risk losing Japanese participation as well. The Chinese government and people were so incensed by the decision to give Japan control over Shantung that, when the German treaty was finally completed, the Chinese delegates refused to sign it.

On April 28, 1919, a little more than three months after the opening of the Peace Conference, the Council of Four submitted the terms of the German treaty to the Plenary Conference. One day later, a 160-member German delegation led by Foreign Minister Count Ulrich von Brockdorff-Rantzau arrived in Paris to receive the draft treaty. For more than a week, the Germans waited impatiently in a heavily guarded hotel near the Palace of Versailles, where the formal signing of the peace settlement was to take place. Finally, at three in the afternoon on May 7, 1919, the German delegation was formally presented with what would come to be known as the Treaty of Versailles. Written in the Peace Conference's two official languages of French and English, the document consisted of 438 articles detailed in some 200 pages and 75,000 words. In presenting the treaty to Count Brockdorff-Rantzau, Clemenceau noted brusquely that the Germans would have two weeks (later extended to three) to submit any comments in writing that they might care to make on the settlement.

By midnight, a preliminary translation of the draft treaty into German had been completed and the count's delegation began to pore through the long document with growing shock and indignation. "This fat volume was quite unnecessary," Brockdorff-Rantzau was heard to observe bitterly: "They could have expressed the whole thing more simply in one clause— 'L'Allemagne renonce à son existence.' (Germany surrenders all claims to its existence.)"[16]

Reaction
to the Treaty

On May 9, Count Ulrich von Brockdorff-Rantzau sent a curt message to Georges Clemenceau, informing him that the German delegation had completed its preliminary review of the draft settlement it had received two days earlier. When the German government had asked Woodrow Wilson to arrange a cease-fire in the autumn of 1918, it had specifically requested that the president's Fourteen Points be the basis for all future peace negotiations between Germany and the Allies. Now, the foreign minister wrote, the Germans felt betrayed. Wilson's peace program had emphasized fairness and reconciliation over punishment and retribution, yet the proposed treaty, Brockdorff-Rantzau asserted, included harsh territorial and financial demands that would be "intolerable for any nation." His delegates, the count concluded angrily, "have been forced to realize that the basis of the peace of justice mutually agreed upon has been abandoned."[1]

Over the next three weeks, the Germans barraged Clemenceau, Wilson, and Lloyd George with notes protesting most of the treaty's provisions, from the occupation of the Rhineland to the loss of the Baltic port of Memel (which eventually went to Lithuania). Article 231—the clause that assigned Germany responsibility for starting the war—particularly angered the delegates. In a series of indignant messages to the Big Three, Brockdorff-Rantzau insisted that Russia had actually sparked the conflict by mobilizing its army in late July 1914, and that the Reich's invasion of France early the following month was not an act of unprovoked aggression, as the Allies accused. Instead, it was a completely justifiable attempt to forestall an invasion by Russia's chief European ally.

THE ALLIES HOLD FIRM

On May 29, Brockdorff-Rantzau presented Clemenceau with a comprehensive list of objections and proposed changes to the draft treaty. At 65,000 words, the count's commentary was nearly as long as the original document itself. Among other things, Brockdorff-Rantzau demanded immediate German admission to the League of Nations; no forced cession of large amounts of German territory to Poland; the elimination of Article 231; and permission for Germany and Austria to unite, which the treaty forbade despite widespread support for unification in both countries. He also complained bitterly about the treaty's provisions regarding reparations. Brockdorff-Rantzau realized that Germany would have to pay some sort of reparations to the Allies. The Germans, after all, had set the precedent for imposing reparations on defeated enemies after the Franco-Prussian War, when they fined France 5 billion francs (a very high sum considering that the war's entire cost was about 2.5 billion francs and virtually all the fighting occurred on French soil). But the Council of Four's decision to form a special commission to set the final amount *after* the treaty had been approved incensed the German delegates. In effect, the

Some members of the German peace delegation informally discuss the peace terms in the park outside of their quarters at Versailles, France. Although the treaty's harsh provisions angered the Germans, they had little choice but to sign or face a renewed Allied assault.

German Republic was being asked to sign a blank check to the Allies, Brockdorff-Rantzau fumed. "No limit is fixed save the capacity of the German people for payment, determined not by their standard of life but solely by their capacity to meet the demands of their enemies by their labor," he accused, concluding that "the German people would thus be condemned to perpetual slave labor."[2]

The German delegation's forceful objections to the treaty worried Lloyd George, who was beginning to have serious doubts regarding Berlin's willingness to approve the document as it stood. After consulting with the rest of the British delegation, Lloyd George decided to press for revisions, including permitting Germany to join the League of Nations at once rather than after a probationary period and shortening the Allied occupation of the Rhineland. Clemenceau and Wilson, however, rebuffed his suggestions for softening some of the treaty's harsher provisions. "We know the Germans better than you," the French Tiger snapped at Lloyd George. "Our concessions will only encourage their resistance while depriving our own peoples of their rights. We do not have to beg pardon for our victory."[3] Although Wilson confided to his press secretary, "If I were a German, I think I should never sign [the treaty]," he was irritated with Lloyd George for waiting to raise his concerns after four long months of negotiations.[4] "The time to consider all these questions," Wilson declared, "was when we were writing the treaty, and it makes me a little tired for people to come and say now that they are afraid the Germans won't sign, and their fear is based upon things that they insisted upon at the time of the writing of the treaty."[5] In the end, Clemenceau and Wilson agreed to just one of Lloyd George's proposals: the mineral-rich and ethnically diverse area in southeastern Germany known as Upper Silesia would not be ceded outright to Poland. Instead, in accordance with the principle of self-determination, the region's inhabitants would be given the opportunity to determine their own future in a plebiscite. (A plebiscite was held in Upper Silesia in 1921. After its results were disputed, the League of Nations intervened and divided the region between Poland and Germany.)

To the frustration of the German delegation, Brockdorff-Rantzau's litany of complaints and counterproposals had no more effect on the final treaty than Lloyd George's objections had had. In the face of German accusations of Allied hypocrisy and greed, the Paris peacemakers simply dug in their heels. When the Germans received the final version of the treaty on June 16, Alan Sharp notes, "the original text had been amended in red ink in a few places."[6] Brockdorff-Rantzau had presented Clemenceau with nearly 200 typewritten pages of criticisms and recommendations on May 29, yet other than some minor changes of wording in several articles and the new provision authorizing a plebiscite in Upper Silesia, the final treaty and the draft treaty were virtually interchangeable. In the cover letter accompanying the document, the Allies warned the German delegation that its government had five days to decide to sign the treaty (later extended to one week) or they would resume military hostilities.

THE GERMANS RESPONDS TO "THE DIKTAT"

Within hours of receiving the treaty, Brockdorff-Rantzau and his chief advisers were on their way to Berlin with the Allied settlement—or the "Diktat" (dictated peace)—as they derisively

THE ALLIES REPLY TO THE GERMAN DELEGATION'S OBJECTIONS TO THE DRAFT TREATY

The following excerpt is from the official Allied response to the German delegation's objections to the draft treaty of May 1919:

The protest of the German Delegation shows that they utterly fail to understand the position in which Germany stands today. They seem to think that Germany has only to "make sacrifices in order to attain peace," as if this were but the end of some mere struggle for territory and power. . . .

In the view of the Allied and Associated Powers the war which began on August 1, 1914, was the greatest crime against humanity and the freedom of peoples that any nation, calling itself civilized, has ever consciously committed.

For many years the rulers of Germany, true to the Prussian tradition, strove for a position of dominance in Europe. . . .

dubbed the document to emphasize that they had had no input in its creation. Convinced that the Allies' threat of renewed military action was merely a bluff, Brockdorff-Rantzau boldly urged German Chancellor Philipp Scheidemann and President Friedrich Ebert to reject it. "The conditions of peace are still unbearable," he declared, "for Germany cannot accept them and continue to live with honor as a nation."[7]

Everyone in the German government from the chancellor and his cabinet to the legislators in the National Assembly

In order to attain their ends they . . . never ceased to expand German armaments by land and sea, and to propagate the falsehood that this was necessary because Germany's neighbours were jealous of her prosperity and power. . . .

They kept Europe in a ferment by threats of violence, and when they found that their neighbours were resolved to resist their arrogant will they determined to assist their predominance in Europe by force.

As soon as their preparations were complete, they encouraged a subservient ally to declare war against Serbia at forty-eight hours' notice, knowing full well that a conflict involving the control of the Balkans could not be localized and almost certainly meant a general war. In order to make doubly sure, they refused every attempt at conciliation and conference until it was too late, and the world war was inevitable for which they had plotted, and for which alone among the nations they were fully equipped and prepared.

Germany's responsibility, however, is not confined to having planned and started the war. She is no less responsible for the savage and inhuman manner in which it was conducted. . . .

(continues)

(continued)

[Germans] were the first to use poisonous gas. . . .
They began the bombing and long distance shelling of
towns for no military object, but solely for the purpose
of reducing the morale of their opponents by striking at
their women and children. They commenced the submarine campaign with its piratical challenge to international
law, and its destruction of great numbers of innocent
passengers and sailors. . . .

That is why the Allied and Associated Powers have
insisted . . . that Germany must undertake to make
reparation to the very uttermost of her power; for reparation for wrongs inflicted is of the essence of justice.
That is why they insist that those individuals who are
most clearly responsible for German aggression and for
those acts of barbarism and inhumanity which have dis-
graced the German conduct of the war, must be handed
over to a justice which has not been meted out to them
at home.

That, too, is why Germany must submit for a few
years to certain special disabilities and arrangements.
Germany has ruined the industries, the mines, and the
machinery of neighboring countries, not during battle,
but with the deliberate and calculated purpose of
enabling her industries to seize their markets before
their industries could recover from the devastation thus
wantonly inflicted upon them. . . .

If these things are hardships for Germany, they are
hardships which Germany has brought upon herself.
Somebody must suffer for the consequences of the war.
Is it to be Germany, or only the peoples she has wronged?*

---

*"Primary Documents: Allied Reply to German Delegates' Protest
Against Proposed Peace Terms at the Paris Peace Conference."
FirstWorldWar.com Web site, http://www.firstworldwar.com/
source/parispeaceconf_germanprotest2.htm.

shared Brockdorff-Rantzau's assessment. The peace terms were humiliating and unjust. Nonetheless, Berlin was deeply divided over what to do about the despised "Diktat." Since the count had failed to produce any evidence to support his claim, many were unconvinced by Brockdorff-Rantzau's assertion that the Allies were bluffing when they pledged to invade Germany should its leaders refuse to sign. Unable to reach a consensus regarding the treaty, Scheidemann and his entire cabinet resigned on June 20, leaving President Ebert to put together a new government just three days before the Allied deadline.

On June 22, after much heated debate, Germany's new chancellor, Gustav Bauer, and his cabinet sent a telegram to Clemenceau stating their willingness to sign the treaty, but with an important qualification: Several particularly offensive articles needed to be removed from the document. These were Article 231, the infamous war-guilt clause, and Article 227 and Article 230, which authorized Allied tribunals to try Kaiser Wilhelm II for "a supreme offense against international morality" and top German military commanders for such "war crimes" as attacking passenger vessels at sea and mistreating prisoners of war.[8] The Big Three's response to Berlin's demand was swift and firm: "The time for discussion is past," they cabled back.[9] Either Germany accepted the treaty as written or Allied invasion forces would begin to cross the Rhine within 24 hours. Convinced they had no choice except to capitulate, Bauer and his cabinet sent a second telegram late on the afternoon of June 23 to Clemenceau informing him that a German delegation would arrive in Versailles within a few days to sign the treaty.

THE TREATY OF VERSAILLES IS CELEBRATED—AND BEMOANED

Clemenceau arranged the signing ceremony for the afternoon of June 28, 1919, the fifth anniversary of the assassination of Archduke Franz Ferdinand in Sarajevo, Bosnia, in the stately Hall of Mirrors at the Palace of Versailles. Since Brockdorff-

On June 28, 1919, a large crowd is present at the Hall of Mirrors during the signing of the Treaty of Versailles, officially ending World War I.

Rantzau had resigned from the foreign ministry shortly after returning to Berlin with the final treaty, Germany was represented by his replacement, Foreign Minister Hermann Müller, and by its minister of transport, Johannes Bell. When Müller and Bell signed the hated treaty, one eyewitness noted that their hands shook slightly, but otherwise they were careful to show no emotion. As soon as the Germans had affixed their signatures to the document, Margaret MacMillan writes, "a signal flashed out from the room to the outside world. Guns around Versailles boomed and the noise spread out to France as other guns took up the chorus."[10] Throughout Paris the waiting crowds roared their approval, and for the rest of the day and well into the night, the city's boulevards and squares overflowed with singing and dancing people, celebrating the official end of the war with Germany.

While Parisians were dancing in the streets on June 28, embittered Germans in towns and cities across the republic were lowering their flags to half-staff, the traditional symbol of mourning. They were particularly dismayed by the war-guilt clause, the Allies' unwillingness to set a definite sum for reparations, and the creation of the Polish Corridor dividing much of eastern Germany from the rest of the nation. They also resented the Allied demand that their former ruler be thrown into jail and tried as a common criminal. (As it turned out, Kaiser Wilhelm II, who fled to neutral Holland in November 1918, was never brought to trial because the Dutch refused to turn him over to the Allies.)

Adding enormously to their displeasure was the wide-spread conviction among Germans that their nation had not been honorably beaten on the battlefield in 1918. Soon after the armistice was signed in November, some German national-ists, including several high-ranking military officers, began to insist that, if the army had been allowed to continue fighting, Germany could have won the war or, at the very least, held the Allies to a standoff. Instead, the nation's traitorous new leaders in Berlin—the liberals and socialists who founded the Weimar Republic—had tricked the German people into believing that Germany had no choice but to surrender. Although the nationalists' theory was pure fabrication, millions of ordinary Germans embraced their version of events. Their willingness to believe such an obvious falsehood probably had much to do with Kaiser Wilhelm II's strict wartime censorship policies—his subjects heard only positive reports from the battlefront. Indeed, right up until the fall of the imperial government dur-ing the conflict's final weeks, the German people were told that victory was imminent. If their army, instead of being defeated

Anti-Versailles demonstrations were widespread across Germany. Here, demonstrators protest the granting of Posen to Poland and the decision to make Danzig a free city in 1920, under the treaty's provisions.

fair and square on the battlefield in 1918, had been betrayed by the new republican regime, many Germans asked, how could the Allies pretend there was any justice in imposing such a punitive settlement on them as the Treaty of Versailles?

OPPOSITION TO THE TREATY IN BRITAIN AND THE UNITED STATES

In the immediate aftermath of World War I, public opinion in Great Britain leaned heavily toward a harsh peace settlement, particularly in the area of reparations. During the months after the treaty officially went into effect in January 1920, however, growing numbers of Britons began to reconsider the treaty's more stringent provisions. The chief reason for their change of heart was *The Economic Consequences of Peace*, a best-selling critique of the peace settlement by John Maynard Keynes, a former economic adviser to the British delegation at Paris.

Published in December 1919, just five months after the British Parliament ratified the treaty, *The Economic Consequences of Peace* savaged the Versailles settlement and its main authors, Wilson, Lloyd George, and especially Clemenceau, whom Keynes portrayed as utterly unreasonable in his determination to impose a "Carthaginian peace" on Germany.[11] (The term *Carthaginian peace* refers to ancient Rome's complete destruction of Carthage after its victory over the African city-state in 146 B.C.) Keynes was particularly critical of the reparations provisions that assigned Germany responsibility for the victorious nations' military pensions and allowances. Saddling the German Republic with heavy reparations, he accused, was vindictive, unjust, and ultimately impractical since it would only serve to hinder the rest of Europe's economic recovery. Despite Keynes's condemnation of the treaty, many historians have noted that, compared with the peace terms Germany imposed on Bolshevik Russia in early 1918, the Versailles settlement appears almost mild. According to the Allied peace settlement, Germany lost about 10 percent of its prewar population and industry and 13 percent of its prewar territory, including Alsace-Lorraine. Yet under the Treaty of Brest-Litovsk of March 1918 between the German Reich and Russia, Russia was to lose 33 percent of its population and industry and 25 percent of its European territory. (The Treaty of Brest-Litovsk was only partially implemented before November 11, 1918, when Germany was forced to renounce the settlement as part of the Allied armistice agreement.)

Accurate or not, Keynes's portrayal of the Treaty of Versailles as vindictive and harsh made a huge impression. *The Economic Consequences of Peace* was released in the United States in early

1920, shortly before the U.S. Senate was to vote for the second time on whether to ratify the treaty. (In November 1919, in a devastating blow to Woodrow Wilson, the Senate failed to approve the Treaty of Versailles by the required two-thirds majority. Just weeks earlier, the president had suffered a massive stroke following a grueling tour of the country to drum up support for the League of Nations, which in his view was by far the most important part of the treaty.) During the winter of 1920, as Wilson lay ill, Keynes's book helped create doubts in the Senate. It also gave important new ammunition to the treaty's opponents, particularly the powerful Republican chairman of the Senate Foreign Relations Committee, Henry Cabot Lodge. Lodge was especially unhappy with Article 10 of the League of Nations covenant, which obliged member states to defend one another "against external aggression."[12] Lodge contended that, if the United States became locked into the collective security system created by the league, it would become entangled in European wars and lose its freedom of action. To address this issue, among the numerous amendments that Lodge sought to add to the treaty was one stipulating that the United States could not engage in any collective security actions without the approval of Congress.

From his sickbed, Wilson, who was adamantly opposed to any changes to the treaty, instructed his fellow Democrats in the Senate to vote against all amendments to the peace settlement. In large measure because of the president's refusal to compromise, the Senate rejected the treaty for the second and final time on March 19, 1920, falling short of the necessary two-thirds majority by just seven votes. Wilson's cherished dream of U.S. participation in the international peace organization that he had done so much to create and on which he pinned such great hopes was dead. In August 1921, nearly six months after Wilson's Republican successor, President Warren G. Harding, took office, the United States signed a separate peace treaty with Germany.

The Peacemakers and Germany's Allies

A lthough the treaty between Germany and the Allies is the most famous settlement to emerge from the Paris Peace Conference, it was not the only one. The Allied peacemakers also drew up separate agreements with Germany's Central Power allies: Austria, Bulgaria, Hungary, and Turkey. These treaties would largely redraw the maps of Eastern and Central Europe and the Middle East with important consequences for the future of those regions.

AUSTRIA RECEIVES THE ALLIED PEACE TERMS

The first of the peace agreements to be concluded between the Allies and the lesser Central Powers was the Austrian treaty. By the time of the June 28, 1919, signing ceremony for the Treaty of Versailles, the Austrian peace settlement had been largely hammered out under the supervision of the Council of Four, and a delegation from Vienna headed by Chancellor Karl Renner was reviewing it.

The Paris peacemakers had formally presented Renner with the draft treaty in early June at the royal palace of St. Germain in the Parisian suburb of the same name. The Austria now represented by Renner and the rest of the Viennese delegation was a very different country from the Austria of just five years earlier. In 1914, the Austrian royal family, the Habsburgs, governed an extensive empire of some 50 million people, comprising the kingdoms of Austria and Hungary as well as parts of what are now Italy, Croatia, Slovenia, Romania, Poland, and the Czech and Slovak Republics. By November 3, 1918, when Austria signed a cease-fire with the Allies, the vast Austro-Hungarian Empire was rapidly disintegrating. A month before the cease-fire, with the Austrian and Hungarian armies gravely weakened after four years of fighting, first the Poles, and then the Czechs and Yugoslavs (Serbs, Croats, and Slovenes) declared their independence. Then on November 1, Hungary announced that it was dissolving its five-decade-long political union with Austria. Two weeks later, Austria ousted its last Habsburg monarch, Emperor Karl I, and proclaimed itself a republic.

The new Austrian Republic claimed ownership over all German-speaking areas of the former Austro-Hungarian Empire, including border regions with Czechoslovakia and Yugoslavia (the area that is now Slovenia). According to the principle of self-determination, Austria's claims to these areas made sense. Yet the Allies were loath to place their former enemy's territorial requests above those of the emerging nations of Czechoslovakia and Yugoslavia, whose inhabitants had fought valiantly with them during the war. Consequently, when the Austrian delegates read the draft treaty in June 1919, they were dismayed to discover that the Allies had awarded the former Austrian region of the Sudetenland to the Czechs, though it was home to some 3 million German speakers, and Carinthia, another largely German area, to Yugoslavia.

Renner and his delegation were also disappointed by the inclusion of an article similar to the one in the Treaty of Versailles forbidding an Austrian-German union (*Anschluss* in German). Before the end of World War I, few Austrians had shown any interest in Anschluss. Their reluctance to unite with Germany was partly rooted in bitter memories of the long Prussian-Austrian rivalry for leadership of Europe's German-speaking peoples and partly in religious differences—Austria was overwhelmingly Roman Catholic while much of Germany was staunchly Protestant. By November 1918, however, with Austria reduced to a fraction of its prewar size and its population and its economy exhausted, many Austrians had changed their minds about Anschluss. They viewed a German-Austrian union, according to Margaret MacMillan, "as the only hope for protection and prosperity for their little country."[1] The Austrian draft treaty also mirrored the German peace settlement on the issue of reparations: Austria would be held responsible for Allied war damages, but the exact amount it owed was to be determined later by a special commission. As it turned out, Austria never paid a cent in reparations. By 1921, the tiny nation's economic situation was so dire that the Reparations Commission decided to waive all Austrian war indemnities.

THE TREATY OF ST. GERMAIN

When Renner's delegation submitted its comments on the draft treaty in late June, the Allies showed more sympathy to the Austrians' objections than they had to German criticisms of the Versailles Treaty. In common with many recent scholars, the Allies considered Germany as the chief instigator and believed Austria had been dragged into the war by its more powerful ally. Although unwilling to back down on the Sudetenland, which the Czechs were particularly eager to possess on account of its numerous textile mills, glassworks, and other factories, the

Allies did make an important concession to Austria concerning the border region of Carinthia. Rather than grant Carinthia outright to Yugoslavia, as the Yugoslavs desired, the Allies agreed to allow the region's mixed Slovene-German population to hold a plebiscite to decide its future. In October 1920, the people of Carinthia voted to remain within Austria.

On the controversial issue of a future Austrian-German union, the Allies also made a concession to the Austrian delegation: The peacemakers revised the treaty to allow Austria to appeal its case to the League of Nations' Executive Council if a majority of the country's population favored Anschluss. This concession, however, was not a meaningful one. According to the league covenant, all decisions of the Executive Council had to be unanimous, and France was adamantly opposed to increasing Germany's territory. Therefore, it was very unlikely that the league would approve a German-Austrian union. In early September, Renner and the Austrian delegation were presented with the revised treaty and told that they had five days to approve it. With the threat of renewed Allied hostilities hanging over them, the Austrians signed the Treaty of St. Germain on September 10, 1919.

THE BULGARIAN TREATY

Bulgaria, the only Balkan nation to join the Central Powers, was the first of Germany's allies to sign an armistice with the Allies on September 29, 1918. Although Bulgaria's army was utterly exhausted by the autumn of 1918, the Slavic nation had achieved some notable successes on the battlefield at the beginning of the conflict, especially against Romania, from which it won the southern portion of the district of Dobrudja on the Black Sea. Romania also claimed southern Dobrudja, but when the Bulgarian delegates arrived in the Parisian suburb of Neuilly in the summer of 1919 to receive their draft treaty from the peacemakers, they were nonetheless optimistic that the Allies would grant them the area. Based on the principle of self-determination, they reasoned, southern Dobrudja should remain within Bulgaria since the majority of the region's population were ethnic Bulgarians.

When the delegates received their copy of the draft treaty in September 1919, they discovered that the Allies had awarded all of Dobrudja to their wartime enemy, Romania. Adding insult to injury, the Allies had also removed western Thrace on the Aegean coast from Bulgarian rule, even though the majority of the region's inhabitants were ethnic Bulgarians. (Eventually western Thrace would be awarded to Greece, which like Romania, had fought on the Allied side in World War I.) According to the treaty's terms, not only was Bulgaria to forfeit 10 percent of its territory, but it would also have to pay reparations of more than $400 million to the Allies. (Bulgaria, its economy in shambles after the war, soon defaulted on the reparations payments.)

Despite strong Bulgarian objections to the territorial provisions of the draft treaty, the Allies refused to back down. Perhaps the Bulgarians would have fared better if Woodrow Wilson, the firmest advocate of self-determination and the sole supporter of their demands for southern Dobrudja and western Thrace in the Council of Four, had still been in Paris during the autumn of 1919. When Wilson (along with Lloyd George) departed Paris for home soon after signing the Treaty of Versailles, Bulgaria was left with no influential supporters at the Peace Conference. Although there was some brave talk about resisting the detested treaty, the country's new prime minister, Alexander Stamboliiski, was too much of a realist to encourage it. On November 27, 1919, Stamboliiski, pale-faced and tense according to one observer, signed the Treaty of Neuilly in a simple ceremony in the town hall of Neuilly.

THE TREATY OF TRIANON

Hungary was also bitterly disappointed by the Allies in 1919. Many of the treaty writers held a highly unfavorable opinion of Hungary. Before World War I, Hungary was reputed to have the most backward and oppressive system of landholding in all of Europe. Although the new republican government in Budapest pledged to institute sweeping land reforms, the aristocratic prime minister, Michael Károlyi, was one of the largest landowners in Hungary and the Allies had little faith in his claim that his country would reform. Hungary's impoverished peasants and workers did not have much faith in Károlyi's promises, either: In March 1919, they overwhelmingly backed the takeover of his government by Béla Kun, a Communist with close ties to the Bolsheviks in Moscow. The Allies were even more leery of Kun than of Károlyi. When the Romanian army, apparently without provocation, invaded Hungary in April, the Allies looked the other way while Romanians troops looted the country for nearly six months. Following the establishment of a new, more conservative regime in Budapest in November 1919, the Allies finally ordered the Romanians to withdraw their forces and summoned a Hungarian delegation to Paris to review the draft treaty.

When the Hungarian delegation, headed by Count Albert Apponyi, arrived in Paris in January 1920, they had few illusions regarding the territorial terms of the settlement since the borders of Hungary's neighbors had largely been determined by this time. Still, they hoped at the very least to be allowed to keep Transylvania, which had been occupied by Romanian troops since the war's end. An extensive region of fertile farmland, lush forests, and rich mineral deposits, Transylvania had been ruled from Budapest more or less since the Middle Ages. To Hungary's dismay, however, the Paris peacemakers placed Transylvania, whose population was more than 50 percent Romanian and only about 25 percent Magyar (the chief Hungarian ethnic group) under Romanian sovereignty. In all, Hungary lost more than two-thirds of its prewar territory and half of its prewar population to its neighbors Romania, Czechoslovakia, and Yugoslavia. It even lost a small strip of land on its western border to Austria, an area claimed by Vienna because most of its inhabitants were German speakers. Despite forfeiting huge amounts of territory, including more than 80 percent of its forests and nearly 50 percent of its farmland, Hungary was still required to pay reparations to its Allied opponents.

In response to the draft treaty, Apponyi pointed out that Hungary was being asked to give up a greater percentage of its prewar territory and population than Austria, Bulgaria, or even Germany. Despite Apponyi's protests, the Hungarian delegation managed to wrest only a few minor concessions from the Allies. The most notable of these was the granting of a plebiscite for the largely Magyar district of Sopron within the western territory that Hungary was to cede to Austria. When the plebiscite was held in December 1921, the city of Sopron voted by a substantial majority to rejoin Hungary.

On June 4, 1920, in a short ceremony in the Grand Trianon Palace at Versailles, Hungarian diplomats reluctantly signed the Treaty of Trianon as government officials back home angrily lowered flags on all public buildings to half-staff. The Hungarian flags would remain at half-staff for nearly 20 years until the humiliated nation finally regained some of the territory it was forced to forfeit with the assistance of a close supporter of Budapest's recently elected fascist regime, Adolf Hitler.

THE ALLIES AND THE OTTOMAN EMPIRE'S MIDDLE EASTERN TERRITORIES

By the Peace Conference's opening, it was evident that the Allies had no intention of allowing the Ottoman Empire, the last of the Central Powers to receive a peace settlement, to retain its Middle Eastern holdings, which included virtually the entire region excepting Iran and Egypt. Britain and France had a longstanding interest in acquiring territory and economic influence in the Middle East, an interest that had grown stronger during the war. The Middle East not only had trade routes linking Europe to India and East Asia, but it also held an abundance of oil. As journalist David A. Andelman points out in *A Shattered Peace: Versailles 1919 and the Price We Pay Today*, World War I was the first war "to highlight the strategic importance of oil." Oil, he writes, "was the fuel for trucks, tanks, ships, and aircraft—all powered by distilled derivatives of the commodity that was just coming to be discovered in the Middle East."[2]

In May 1916, while the war was raging, France and Britain quietly divided most of the Middle East into spheres of influence through the Sykes-Picot Agreement. According to the secret agreement, France would receive Syria and what would become the modern nation of Lebanon, and Britain most of Mesopotamia (part of present-day Iraq) and the Mediterranean ports of Haifa and Akka, after the Ottomans were defeated. Woodrow Wilson was not the only one to express indignation when details of the covert pact, which so blatantly conflicted with his principle of "open covenants of peace, openly arrived at," leaked out in late 1917.[3] Arab leaders in the Middle East were also incensed by the secret treaty, particularly because it conflicted with wartime promises made by the British high commissioner in Egypt, Sir Henry McMahon, to Emir Ali ibn Hussein, head of one of the Arabian Peninsula's most powerful families. In several letters to Hussein during 1915 and 1916, McMahon had implied that, with certain exceptions, Britain would back the founding of an independent Arab state or states in all former Ottoman territories requested by the emir. McMahon's pledge was offered in return for the assistance of the emir's Bedouin warriors in the Allies' Middle Eastern military campaign against the Ottomans, a campaign almost entirely fought by British troops since the French army was tied up on the Western Front.

Further complicating the situation, the British were also committing to another group with a deep interest in the region,

Faisal, who would later be king of Syria and Iraq, with his delegates and advisors at the Versailles Peace Conference in 1919. Behind him, from left to right, are his private secretary Rustem Haidar; Brigadier General Nuri Said of Baghdad; Captain Rosario Pisani of France; Colonel T.E. Lawrence (better known as Lawrence of Arabia) of Great Britain; an unidentified servant; and Hassan Kadri.

the Zionists. Launched in the late nineteenth century when Europe's Jewish population faced rising persecution, Zionism was a worldwide movement to reestablish a Jewish homeland in the ancient Hebrew kingdom of Israel, later known as Palestine, an area whose population had been overwhelmingly Arab for more than 10 centuries. In November 1917, the British foreign secretary, Arthur Balfour, who along with Prime Minister

Lloyd George deeply sympathized with the Zionists, issued his famous Balfour Declaration supporting the settlement of Palestine by the descendents of its ancient Hebrew inhabitants. The British government, Balfour announced, "views with favor the establishment in Palestine of a national home for the Jewish people, and will use their best endeavors to facilitate the achievement of this object."[4] The Balfour Declaration outraged many Arab leaders, who viewed it as yet another Western betrayal to the Arab independence movement.

Despite strong Arab protests, the European Allies publicly backed the Balfour Declaration in April 1920. With the exception of the Arabian Peninsula, where they recognized Arab self-rule, the Middle East was divided between France and Britain very much along the lines of the Sykes-Picot Agreement. France was formally assigned a mandate (or protectorship) over Syria and Lebanon, and Great Britain was given mandates over Mesopotamia, Palestine (present-day Israel, Gaza, and the West Bank), and what is now the nation of Jordan. Two years later, the League of Nations formally sanctioned Britain and France's Middle Eastern mandates.

THE TURKISH HEARTLAND AND THE TREATY OF SÈVRES

In early 1918, Wilson and Lloyd George had publicly implied that, when the fighting was over, Turkey would retain sovereignty over its heartland: the Anatolian peninsula in western Asia and the southeastern tip of the Balkans in Europe, including the port city of Constantinople (now Istanbul). Yet when the Allies in Paris at last got around to discussing Turkey in earnest during the spring and summer of 1919, it quickly became evident that the defeated Ottomans were likely to lose a great deal more territory than their non-Turkish provinces in the Middle East.

In the southern Balkans, Turkey had hoped to be awarded most of the region of Thrace, even though Bulgaria had ruled

Pictured, the signing of the Turkish treaty, the Treaty of Sèvres, with the Allies in August 1920. Because of the Turkish War of Independence, the treaty was never enforced and the parties instead ratified the superseding Treaty of Lausanne in 1923.

Thrace's western portion since 1913. Instead, when the draft treaty with Turkey was finally completed in late April 1920, the Turkish government was dismayed to find that the peacemakers had placed Thrace, with its mixed Turkish-Greek-Bulgarian population, under the control of Greece. Wilson had been adamantly opposed to giving all of Thrace to Greece, but by the spring of 1920, the Treaty of Versailles had been defeated in the U.S. Senate and the United States had largely withdrawn from European affairs. On the Anatolian peninsula, the Allied treaty writers further favored the Greeks by giving them control over the busy Aegean port city of Smyrna (modern-day Izmir), which had a large ethnic Greek population. Promised a share of the Ottoman Empire in the secret Treaty of London in 1915,

Italy was also awarded a sphere of influence along Anatolia's western coast as well as the Dodecanese Islands in the Aegean. Additionally, the draft treaty stipulated that the strategically important Bosphorus and Dardanelles straits, the narrow channels between the southeastern tip of the Balkans and Anatolia that controlled access to the Black Sea, were to be placed under international administration and demilitarized.

Turkish reaction to the draft treaty's severe territorial provisions, particularly concerning Anatolia, was swift and angry. By June 1920, under increasing assault by Turkish militant groups, the Greek occupying army at Smyrna had begun to move inland. With Greece expanding its military presence in Anatolia and Allied forces occupying Constantinople, Turkish Sultan Mehmed VI decided to accept the Allies' terms. On August 10, 1920, Turkish delegates signed the treaty at Sèvres near Paris. As it turned out, however, the treaty would never be enforced.

FROM THE TREATY OF SÈVRES TO THE TREATY OF LAUSANNE

The failure of the Treaty of Sèvres must be largely credited to a Turkish war hero named Mustafa Kemal (later known as Kemal Atatürk). Even before the treaty was signed, the charismatic and brilliant military officer and politician had emerged as the leader of Turkey's growing anti-Allied and pronationalist movement. In 1920, Atatürk established a provisional government in Ankara in central Anatolia and assembled a large nationalist army to free the Turkish heartland from all foreign occupation forces. After a series of battles with the Greek forces on Anatolia, Atatürk's National Army retook Smyrna and pushed the Greeks off the peninsula altogether in September 1922. Atatürk's successful military campaign against the Greeks persuaded the rest of the Allies, who had no desire to become bogged down in a war in Turkey, to renegotiate a peace settlement with the former Central Power. Since the Paris Peace

KEMAL ATATÜRK AND WESTERN DEMOCRATIC TRADITIONS

On October 29, 1923, after officially abolishing the Ottoman sultanate, Kemal Atatürk became the founder and first president of the new Turkish Republic. Over the next 15 years (until his death in 1938), Atatürk instituted a series of cultural, social, legal, educational, economic, and political reforms, most of them based on Western models. Through his sweeping modernization program, Atatürk sought above

all to strengthen his homeland, which he feared was being surpassed by more advanced Western nations in virtually every field.

In the realm of political reform, Atatürk was determined to remake Turkey, an autocratic theocracy under the Ottoman sultanate, in the image of a Western-style democracy. In deference to democratic principles,

Mustafa Kemal Atatürk and his wife, Latifee Hanoun, in the garden of their villa near Ankara, circa 1923.

(continues)

(continued)

he backed the adoption of a full republican constitution for Turkey; the formation of a popularly elected legislature, the unicameral Grand National Assembly; women's suffrage; expanded educational opportunities for all Turks; and the total separation of religion and state. Yet if Atatürk incorporated many democratic elements into Turkey's new political system, in the name of national security he shrank from adopting one of the most fundamental principles of Western-style democracy: political pluralism. Throughout most of his 15 years as Turkey's chief executive, he allowed no organized opposition to his own political party, the Republican People's Party. Consequently, with few exceptions, the Grand National Assembly simply rubber-stamped Atatürk's initiatives, even granting him sweeping emergency powers in 1926 to go after his political opponents—many of whom were exiled or imprisoned—after a plot against his life by a former aide was uncovered. Even though Atatürk's insistence on single-party rule clearly conflicted with traditional democratic principles, under his successors the modern Turkish state he helped to create would eventually evolve into what many scholars have characterized as one of the most genuinely democratic nations in western Asia.

Conference had long since disbanded, a new peace conference was assembled in Lausanne, Switzerland, in late 1922—this time with Turkish as well as Allied negotiators present, at the insistence of Atatürk.

On July 24, 1923, the Swiss peace conference produced the Treaty of Lausanne, which did not give Turkey everything its leaders sought. Most significantly, the settlement permitted Greece to retain western Thrace. Although it returned administration of the Bosphorus and Dardanelles straits to Turkey, the treaty stipulated that the straits remain demilitarized and open to international shipping. Nonetheless, the Treaty of Lausanne did award Turkey eastern Thrace in the Balkans, the entire Anatolian peninsula, parts of neighboring Armenia, and numerous Aegean islands. Perhaps more importantly, no restrictions were placed on the Turkish military, while the Treaty of Sèvres had severely reduced the Ottoman army and navy and prohibited the country from developing an air force. By the time the Treaty of Lausanne was signed, the post-World War I peacemaking process had been going on for four and a half years. The effects of the peacemakers' decisions from January 1919 to July 1923, however, were destined to last for many years to come.

The Peacemakers' Legacy

Traditionally, the burdensome financial, military, and territorial terms of the Treaty of Versailles have been blamed for the rise of Adolf Hitler and fascism in Germany. A growing number of modern scholars, however, reject the view that the treaty's more stringent provisions pushed Germany toward Nazism. The only major connection between the Versailles settlement and the rise of Nazism, they argue, was Hitler's genius for exploiting the unpopular treaty's propaganda value. Throughout the 1920s and 1930s, Hitler found the treaty a useful rhetorical tool for rallying public opinion behind his ultranationalistic and antidemocratic movement, even after many of the peace settlement's terms had been revised in Germany's favor.

THE POSTWAR REPARATIONS CONTROVERSY

Of all the treaty's various provisions, its financial clauses have earned the most blame for swaying German public opinion toward Nazism. According to traditional interpretation of the treaty's impact on Germany, the Weimar Republic's efforts to meet its reparations obligations during the early 1920s plunged the nation into an economic free fall. Angered and frightened by the escalating economic crisis and the social unrest that accompanied it, growing numbers of Germans came to view Hitler's authoritarian and nationalistic movement as the answer to their country's woes. In recent years, however, some economists and historians have challenged the notion that the reparations' effect on the German economy helped pave the way for Hitler. These revisionist scholars note that while the amount set by the international Reparations Commission in April 1921—132 billion gold marks (about $33 billion)—was high, it should have been manageable for Berlin since the German economy was still one of the world's largest. That Berlin had fallen behind on its financial obligations by the end of 1922 was not because the indemnities were too burdensome, these scholars argue; rather it was because German leaders viewed reparations as humiliating and unjust and therefore sought to put off paying them as long as possible.

In January 1923, French troops assisted by a token Belgian force occupied the Ruhr, Germany's chief industrial district, in hopes of forcing Berlin to pay up. Resolved not to give in to French military pressure, nationalistic German political and business leaders "coordinated a campaign of passive resistance," Ruth Henig writes, and throughout the Ruhr, "industrial production ground to a halt."[1] With the nation's coal and steel output severely reduced, the value of the German mark sank rapidly against the U.S. dollar. Berlin responded to the mark's dramatic depreciation by pumping massive amounts of paper money into the nation's economy. As a result, hyperinflation created exorbitant prices for food and other necessities, which caused widespread suffering and discontent throughout the republic. The effects of Germany's monetary crisis soon spread to the rest of Europe, especially France, where the franc depreciated by 25 percent.

By 1924, U.S. leaders were so concerned about Europe's economic troubles that they decided to intervene in the reparations controversy, even though Washington had largely withdrawn from the continent's affairs after the Senate's rejection

HITLER DENOUNCES THE TREATY OF VERSAILLES

On April 7, 1923, during a rally in Munich, an up-and-coming German politician named Adolf Hitler gave a vitriolic speech on the injustice of the Treaty of Versailles and the cowardice of the Weimar politicians who had approved it. Over the next decade and a half, until the outbreak of World War II in the summer of 1939, the ultranationalistic Hitler repeatedly denounced the peace settlement to his fellow Germans in impassioned terms. Here is an excerpt from the 1923 speech:

> With the armistice begins the humiliation of Germany. If the Republic on the day of its foundation had appealed to the country: Germans, stand together! Up and resist the foe! The Fatherland, the Republic expects of you that you fight to your last breath, then millions who are now enemies of the Republic would be fanatical Republicans. Today they are the foes of the Republic not because it is a Republic but because this Republic was founded at the moment when Germany was humiliated, because it so discredited the new flag that men's eyes must turn regretfully toward the old

of the Versailles Treaty. During the winter and spring of 1924, American financial experts helped formulate the Dawes Plan, a revised German reparations program that established a less demanding yearly repayment schedule for Berlin. Five years later, German reparations were revised again in Berlin's favor by the Young Plan, which reduced the country's debt to the Allies to 121 billion marks. By the time the new plan was scheduled to take effect in late 1930, however, the U.S. stock market crash of October 1929 had triggered a severe economic downturn throughout the world. In response to the Great Depression, the

flag. So long as this Treaty stands there can be no resurrection of the German people; no social reform of any kind is possible! The Treaty was made in order to bring 20 million Germans to their deaths and to ruin the German nation. As its foundation our Movement formulated three demands:

1. Setting aside of the Peace Treaty.
2. Unification of all Germans.
3. Land and soil [Grund und Boden] to feed our nation.

Our movement could formulate these demands, since it was not our Movement which caused the War, it has not made the Republic, it did not sign the Peace Treaty.

There is thus one thing which is the first task of this Movement: it desires to make the German once more National, that his Fatherland shall stand for him above everything else. It desires to teach our people to understand afresh the truth of the old saying: He who will not be a hammer must be an anvil. An anvil we are today, and that anvil will be beaten until out of the anvil we fashion once more a hammer, a German sword!*

---

*"The Great War: Evaluating the Treaty of Versailles," http://edsitement.neh.gov/lesson_images/lesson424/Hitlerspeech.pdf.

A circa 1920 picture from famine-stricken Austria showing boys tramping home with firewood in the Brennholtz, outside of Vienna. Most historians now agree that postwar Austrian and German economic troubles cannot be blamed on the reparations set by the Treaty of Versailles.

international Lausanne Conference temporarily suspended all German reparations payments in 1932.

All told, the Allies received just 36 billion marks in reparations from the German government. Of that amount, all but 3 billion marks came from foreign—mostly American—loans. Berlin officially defaulted on these loans in 1933, the year Hitler became chancellor. Because Berlin failed to make good on the loans, German taxpayers ultimately paid only about 2 percent of the 121-billion-mark indemnity set by the Young Plan, making the "actual effect of reparations" on postwar Germany "economically negligible," Charles Mee observes.[2] The fact that Germany managed to evade paying the bulk of its reparations, Mee and other recent scholars of the Versailles settlement contend, provides indisputable evidence that the

German Republic's postwar economic troubles—and the pro-Nazi sentiment those troubles helped engender among the German people—were not the fault of the Paris peacemakers, as has often been alleged.

THE ABANDONMENT OF THE VERSAILLES SETTLEMENT AND THE COMING OF WORLD WAR II

By 1935, with the fiercely nationalistic Hitler now führer (supreme leader) of the Nazi Third Reich, Berlin renounced most of its military requirements along with its financial obligations under the Versailles Treaty. From the start, the Allies had fought an uphill battle to compel Germany to adhere to the treaty's disarmament clauses. After all, Berlin pointed out, the Allies were making no concerted effort to disarm themselves, even though voluntary international disarmament was supposed to closely follow German disarmament.

On March 7, 1936, Hitler, having expanded the German army well beyond what the treaty allowed, marched his troops into the Rhineland in violation of Articles 42 and 43, which prohibited German military personnel or fortifications from being placed there. Neither Britain nor France, the treaty's main guarantors since the early 1920s, made any effort to force the German army out of the Rhineland. (The other two Allied powers, the United States and Italy, were not involved with guaranteeing the treaty because the U.S. Senate had not ratified the settlement and Italy had fallen under the control of Hitler's ally, the fascist dictator Benito Mussolini.) Preoccupied with maintaining their nation's position as the world's leading power, British leaders had no desire to become entangled in a distracting and potentially expensive fight with Germany. Unwilling to take on the increasingly powerful Third Reich on its own, France focused instead on strengthening its Maginot Line, massive concrete and steel fortifications that the French army had started to build on the German frontier in 1930, when the last Allied occupation troops vacated the Rhineland.

German soldiers cross the Cologne Bridge during Germany's reoccupation of the Rhineland in 1936, in direct violation of the Treaty of Versailles.

The League of Nations was also of little help in this latest—and most serious—controversy regarding enforcement of the treaty. The international peacekeeping organization lacked the political and military clout to reign in aggressor nations, as its inability to stop Japan from occupying Manchuria in northeastern China or Italy from invading Ethiopia during the early and mid-1930s had clearly demonstrated.

The fact that the Allies did nothing while Hitler remilitarized the Rhineland encouraged him to violate other provisions of the Versailles settlement. In early 1938, Nazi troops marched into Vienna to enforce the unification of Austria and Germany, something expressly forbidden by the Paris peacemakers and strongly opposed by the Austrian government.

When the international community once again shrank from taking action against Germany, Hitler boldly ordered his troops into Czechoslovakia's Sudetenland region. The Sudetenland had never belonged to Germany, but since its inhabitants were predominantly German speakers, Hitler accused the peacemakers of unjustly awarding the former Austrian territory to Czechoslovakia in 1919. Wary of Hitler from the start, the Czechs had, in the mid-1930s, built a vast system of fortifications in the mountainous Sudetenland as protection against German invasion. Thus, when Hitler demanded that Czechoslovakia turn over the Sudetenland to the Third Reich, Czech leaders were understandably worried that losing their heavily fortified border region would put the independence of the entire nation in jeopardy.

In response to this newest crisis, France and Britain called up their armies for the first time since World War I. Nevertheless, anxious to avoid a military conflict, French and British leaders sought to appease Hitler at the Munich Conference of September 1938 by giving him the Sudetenland in return for his pledge that Germany would make no further territorial demands on its neighbors. Six months later, Hitler reneged on the Munich Agreement and ordered German troops to occupy the rest of Czechoslovakia. After Nazi forces invaded Poland on September 1, 1939, ostensibly to recover the former German territories of the Polish Corridor and the port city of Danzig, Britain and France at last declared war on the Third Reich. Just two decades after German and Allied delegates officially concluded the "war to end all wars" by signing the Treaty of Versailles, Europe was plunged into another world war, a cataclysm even more deadly and destructive than the first had been.

THE PEACEMAKERS' LEGACY IN EASTERN AND CENTRAL EUROPE AND THE MIDDLE EAST

One chief criticism of the Treaty of Versailles, voiced not only by Hitler but also by numerous commentators in the decades after World War II, concerned the agreement's territorial provisions for Eastern and Central Europe. In setting new national borders following the disintegration of the Austro-Hungarian Empire, critics asserted, the peacemakers strayed from Woodrow Wilson's ideal of self-determination, particularly when they were dealing with Germans. According to this principle, the treaty writers should not have assigned the predominantly German-speaking territories of the Sudetenland and the Polish Corridor to Czechoslovakia and Poland, respectively. As historian William Keylor argues in the Allies' defense, however, drawing postwar Europe's boundaries on the basis of ethnicity alone "would have had the paradoxical consequence of significantly strengthening the German state by authorizing it to expand its national territory far beyond the frontiers of [Otto von] Bismarck's Reich."[3]

Regarding the peacemakers' controversial role in reshaping Eastern Europe, some critics have even accused the Allies of laying the foundations for the ethnic violence that led to the disintegration of Yugoslavia in the 1990s. Yet the idea for establishing a large, ethnically diverse Yugoslav (literally "southern Slav") state in the Balkans did not originate with the Allies. Instead, just as the Czechs and Slovaks themselves were the first to press for the establishment of Czechoslovakia (now the Czech Republic and the Slovak Republic), it was Serb, Croat, and Slovene leaders, not the Paris negotiators, who invented Yugoslavia. Concerned above all with building a politically and economically viable Slavic state, Croats, Serbs, and Slovenes willingly put aside old grievances and prejudices and united under one government in 1918.

In the Middle East, however, the Allies' creation of new nations with little regard for the wishes of the region's indigenous populations sowed the seeds for generations of strife. Many commentators consider the French mandate of Lebanon and the two British mandates of Palestine and Mesopotamia as the Allies' most egregious errors in reshaping the postwar

Middle East. Rather than consider the desires of the diverse inhabitants of the former Ottoman territories, the French and British thought only of their own economic and geopolitical goals. In the tiny administrative unit of Lebanon, previously part of a much bigger Ottoman province dominated by Muslim Syria, Paris merged one of the Middle East's largest Christian communities with several smaller Muslim settlements, hoping to create a reliably pro-French state. When Lebanon finally gained its independence during the 1940s, Lebanese Christians, consistently favored over Muslims by the former mandate's French administrators, quickly came to dominate the new national government to the dismay of the rapidly growing Muslim minority. In 1975, with followers of Islam now in the majority in Lebanon, the country's longstanding religious rivalries boiled over into a destructive civil war pitting Christian against Muslim, the roots of which can be largely traced to the arbitrary borders set by the Allies decades before.

The Allied treaty writers had assembled Palestine from three separate Ottoman administrative units. There, the British struggled for more than a quarter of a century to persuade Arabs and Jews to live together peacefully before finally pulling out of the increasingly volatile region in 1948. The founding of the Jewish State of Israel in the former British mandate in May 1948 produced enormous resentment among the Middle East's Muslim majority. Over the years, that resentment came to be directed not only at the Israelis, but also at the British government for interfering in Palestine in the first place and at the American government for providing crucial economic, political, and military support to Israel.

In the British mandate of Mesopotamia, as in Lebanon and Palestine, the Allies threw together disparate and traditionally antagonistic populations when they united several former Ottoman provinces: Basra, a Shiite Muslim enclave; Sunni Muslim-dominated Baghdad; and Mosul, where a non-Arabic people, the Kurds, were in the majority. Following a series of bloody uprisings by Shiites and Sunnis against the mandatory government, the British awarded self-rule to Mesopotamia in 1921, soon to be renamed Iraq. A series of authoritarian

GERTRUDE BELL: PIONEER FEMALE DIPLOMAT

The only woman to play a key role in the Allied peace settlements, Gertrude Bell (1868-1926) of Great Britain was one of only a small number of female diplomats during the early twentieth century. Highly educated and adventurous, Bell had traveled extensively in the Middle East before the war and particularly in Iraq, then the Ottoman provinces of Mosul, Baghdad, and Basra, and quickly became fluent in the Arabic language. In 1917, the British government recruited Bell to serve as Oriental Secretary to Percy Cox, the top British political officer in Baghdad. Two years later, she became one of a handful of female diplomats to attend the Paris Peace Conference when she accompanied Prince Faisal, son of the powerful Arabian leader Ali ibn Hussein, to France to discuss the future of Turkey's former Mesopotamian provinces.

After the Allied peacemakers assigned the mandate for all of Mesopotamia to Great Britain in accordance with London's wishes, Bell became one of the most influential British diplomats in the Middle East, serving as chief assistant to the high commissioner, Sir Arnold Wilson. Dismayed by Wilson's authoritarian governing style, Bell was not surprised when a series of violent uprisings against British rule erupted in Mosul and the Euphrates valley during the summer of 1920. A few months earlier, she had written a controversial report recommending that Britain end

leaders held Iraq together until the early twenty-first century, when U.S.-led coalition forces toppled Saddam Hussein, Iraq's brutal dictator, in 2003. Shortly after Hussein's fall, widespread

Ibn Saud, the future King of Saudi Arabia, meets with British diplomat Sir Percy Cox *(center)* and Gertrude Bell.

its increasingly unpopular mandate over Mesopotamia and institute self-rule there as soon as possible. In March 1921, Bell became the only woman invited by British Colonial Secretary Winston Churchill to attend the Cairo Conference on the problems then facing Britain in the Middle East, including how to go about giving Mesopotamia its independence. At the meeting she played a central role in drawing the borders of the new Mesopotamian kingdom, soon to be renamed Iraq, and in persuading Churchill to install her friend Prince Faisal as the fledgling country's first ruler in August 1921.

sectarian violence between Shiites and Sunnis erupted. Nearly nine decades after Allied diplomats first joined together Basra, Baghdad, and Mosul, the people of the three former Ottoman provinces had yet to truly coalesce into a nation.

Perhaps no other international agreements have aroused as much controversy or been analyzed as thoroughly as the Treaty of Versailles and the other peace settlements of World War I. Few would dispute that the Allied peacemakers made serious mistakes in the Middle East, where they created new nations with little appreciation for the particular religious beliefs, ethnic backgrounds, and histories of the diverse peoples whom they so cavalierly joined together. On the other hand, although the financial and territorial terms the treaty writers imposed on Germany and its European allies have been widely criticized over the years, today their efforts to fashion a more stable and peaceful order in the West are viewed more sympathetically. Alan Sharp notes that, for the Versailles Treaty's authors, "there was a deadline; decisions had to be taken, on countless individual occasions, with imperfect information, under pressure, frequently when those responsible were both mentally and physically exhausted. And then the next decision had to be taken, probably on a new, apparently unrelated topic, and this went on day after day in an unremitting round."[4]

In May 1919, before the Treaty of Versailles was formally presented to the German delegation, one of the document's principal authors rendered his own verdict on the just completed yet already highly controversial agreement. "Above all else it is the work of human beings and, as a result, it is not perfect," mused Georges Clemenceau.[5] Faced with the monumental task of bringing order to a world shattered by four years of war and divided by fierce hatreds and competing aspirations, Clemenceau believed that, in the end, he and the other Paris peacemakers had done the best they could.

CHRONOLOGY

1914   **August** World War I begins, pitting the Central Powers of Austria-Hungary and Germany against the Allies led by Russia, Great Britain, and France.

October Turkish Ottoman Empire joins the Central Powers.

1915   **May** Italy enters the war on the Allied side.

1917   **April** United States declares war on Germany and enters World War I.

October The Bolshevik Revolution occurs in Russia.

1918   **January** President Woodrow Wilson announces his Fourteen Points.

March Russia signs the Treaty of Brest-Litovsk with Germany.

November Armistice is reached between the Allies and Germany.

1919   **January** The Paris Peace Conference opens.

June The treaty with Germany is signed in the Hall of Mirrors at the Palace of Versailles.

September Austrians sign the Treaty of St. Germain.

November Bulgarians sign the Treaty of Neuilly.

1920   **January** The Treaty of Versailles officially comes into force.

March U.S. Senate fails to approve the Treaty of Versailles.

June Hungarians sign the Treaty of Trianon.

August Turks sign the Treaty of Sèvres.

1921   **April** Reparations Commission sets payments for Germany at 132 billion marks.

               August United States signs Treaty of Berlin with Germany.

1923   **January** French troops occupy the Ruhr after Germany falls behind on reparations.

               July The Treaty of Lausanne is signed with Turkey.

1924   **April** Dawes Plan to revise Germany's reparations payment schedule is approved.

1929   **August** Young Plan to reduce German reparations payments is approved.

TIMELINE

August 1914
World War I begins.

January 1918
President Woodrow Wilson announces his Fourteen Points.

1914   1919

April 1917
United States enters World War I on Allied side.

November 1918
Armistice between Allies and Germany.

January 1919
Paris Peace Conference opens.

1930   June Last Allied troops leave the Rhineland five
        years ahead of date set in treaty.

1932   July Reparations payments from Germany are
        suspended by the Lausanne Agreement.

1933   January Adolf Hitler becomes German chancellor
        and defaults on foreign loans.

1936   March Hitler remilitarizes the Rhineland.

1939   September German troops invade Poland,
        starting World War II.

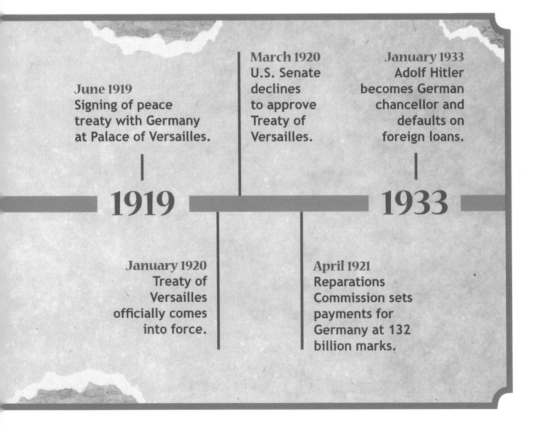

June 1919
Signing of peace
treaty with Germany
at Palace of Versailles.

March 1920
U.S. Senate
declines
to approve
Treaty of
Versailles.

January 1933
Adolf Hitler
becomes German
chancellor and
defaults on
foreign loans.

1919

1933

January 1920
Treaty of
Versailles
officially comes
into force.

April 1921
Reparations
Commission sets
payments for
Germany at 132
billion marks.

NOTES

CHAPTER 1

1. Justin Ewers, "Versailles Revised; Think that the Treaty of Versailles Led to World War II? Think Again." *U.S. News & World Report*, December 2, 2002, p. 44.
2. Margaret MacMillan, *Paris 1919: Six Months That Changed the World*. New York: Random House, 2001, p. 493.

CHAPTER 2

1. Alan Sharp, *The Versailles Settlement: Peacemaking in Paris, 1919*. New York: St. Martin's Press, 1991, pp. 2–3.
2. David Fromkin, *Europe's Last Summer: Who Started the Great War in 1914?* New York: Alfred A. Knopf, 2004, p. 245.
3. Frank McDonough, *The Origins of the First and Second World Wars*. Cambridge, United Kingdom: Cambridge University Press, 1997, p. 24.
4. Ruth B. Henig, *Versailles and After, 1919–1933*. London: Routledge, 1995, p. 21.
5. Fromkin, *Europe's Last Summer*, pp. 266–267.
6. Robin Prior, Trevor Wilson, and John Keegan, *The First World War*. London: Cassell, 1999, pp. 26–27.

CHAPTER 3

1. Joe H. Kirchberger, *The First World War: An Eyewitness History*. New York: Facts on File, 1992, p. 81.
2. Sharp, *The Versailles Settlement*, p. 11.
3. Edward Mandell House, *The Intimate Papers of Colonel House Arranged as a Narrative by Charles Seymour*. 4 vols. New York: Houghton Mifflin, 1926–1928, vol. ii, p. 412.
4. Thomas J. Knock, *To End All Wars: Woodrow Wilson and the Quest for a New World Order*. New York: Oxford University Press, 1992, p. 121.
5. Charles L. Mee, Jr., *The End of Order: Versailles 1919*. New York: E.P. Dutton, 1980, p. 11.
6. Henig, *Versailles and After*, p. 76.
7. MacMillan, *Paris 1919*, p. 33.
8. Mee, *The End of Order*, p. 12.

CHAPTER 4

1. Ibid., p. 48.
2. MacMillan, *Paris 1919*, p. 31.
3. Ibid., p. 28.
4. Henig, *Versailles and After*, p. 2.
5. Mee, *The End of Order*, p. 58.
6. MacMillan, *Paris 1919*, p. 85.
7. Sharp, *The Versailles Settlement*, p. 55.
8. MacMillan, *Paris 1919*, p. 91.
9. Sharp, *The Versailles Settlement*, pp. 65, 67, 70.

CHAPTER 5

1. MacMillan, *Paris 1919*, p. 176.
2. Henig, *Versailles and After*, p. 19.

3. Knock, *To End All Wars*, p. 144.

4. Henig, *Versailles and After*, p. 19.

5. Knock, *To End All Wars*, p. 250.

6. Sharp, *The Versailles Settlement*, p. 87.

7. Henig, *Versailles and After*, p. 21.

8. Knock, *To End All Wars*, p. 248.

9. MacMillan, *Paris 1919*, p. 200.

10. Ibid., p. 169.

11. Sharp, *The Versailles Settlement*, p. 120.

12. MacMillan, *Paris 1919*, p. 197.

13. Henig, *Versailles and After*, p. 24.

14. Ibid., p. 26.

15. Knock, *To End All Wars*, p. 250.

16. MacMillan, *Paris 1919*, p. 465.

CHAPTER 6

1. Ferdinand Czernin, *Versailles, 1919: The Forces, Events and Personalities That Shaped the Treaty*. New York: G.P. Putnam's Sons, 1964, p. 35.

2. MacMillan, *Paris 1919*, p. 192.

3. Mee, *The End of Order*, p. 236.

4. Ann Hagedorn, *Savage Peace: Hope and Fear in America, 1919*. New York: Simon & Schuster, 2007, p. 264.

5. Mee, *The End of Order*, p. 238.

6. Sharp, *The Versailles Settlement*, p. 38.

7. MacMillan, *Paris 1919*, p. 473.

8. Sharp, *The Versailles Settlement*, p. 126.

9. Mee, *The End of Order*, p. 251.

10. MacMillan, *Paris 1919*, p. 476.

11. Sharp, *The Versailles Settlement*, p. 194.

12. Ibid., p. 67.

CHAPTER 7

1. MacMillan, *Paris 1919*, p. 252.

2. David A. Andelman, *A Shattered Peace: Versailles 1919 and the Price We Pay Today*. Hoboken, N.J.: John Wiley & Sons, 2007, p. 49.

3. Henig, *Versailles and After*, p. 75.

4. David Fromkin, *A Peace to End All Peace: The Fall of the Ottoman Empire and the Creation of the Modern Middle East*. New York: Macmillan, 2001, p. 297.

CHAPTER 8

1. Henig, *Versailles and After*, p. 36.

2. Mee, *The End of Order*, p. 261.

3. William R. Keylor, "Versailles and International Diplomacy," in Manfred F. Boemeke, Gerald D. Feldman, and Elisabeth Gläser, eds., *The Treaty of Versailles: A Reassessment After 75 Years*. Cambridge, United Kingdom: Cambridge University Press, 1998, p. 492.

4. Sharp, *The Versailles Settlement*, p. 185.

5. MacMillan, *Paris 1919*, p. 460.

BIBLIOGRAPHY

Andelman, David A. *A Shattered Peace: Versailles 1919 and the Price We Pay Today.* Hoboken, N.J.: John Wiley & Sons, 2007.

Boemeke, Manfred F., Gerald D. Feldman, and Elisabeth Gläser, eds. *The Treaty of Versailles: A Reassessment After 75 Years.* Cambridge, United Kingdom: Cambridge University Press, 1998.

Cooper, John Milton, Jr. *Breaking the Heart of the World: Woodrow Wilson and the Fight for the League of Nations.* Cambridge, United Kingdom: Cambridge University Press, 2001.

Czernin, Ferdinand. *Versailles, 1919: The Forces, Events and Personalities That Shaped the Treaty.* New York: G.P. Putnam's Sons, 1964.

Ewers, Justin. "Versailles Revised; Think that the Treaty of Versailles Led to World War II? Think Again." *U.S. News & World Report,* December 2, 2002, p. 44.

Fromkin, David. *Europe's Last Summer: Who Started the Great War in 1914?* New York: Alfred A. Knopf, 2004.

———. *A Peace to End All Peace: The Fall of the Ottoman Empire and the Creation of the Modern Middle East.* New York: Macmillan, 2001.

Hagedorn, Ann. *Savage Peace: Hope and Fear in America, 1919.* New York: Simon & Schuster, 2007.

Henig, Ruth B. *Versailles and After, 1919–1933.* London: Routledge, 1995.

House, Edward Mandell. *The Intimate Papers of Colonel House Arranged as a Narrative by Charles Seymour.* 4 vols. New York: Houghton Mifflin, 1926–1928.

Kirchberger, Joe H. *The First World War: An Eyewitness History.* New York: Facts on File, 1992.

Knock, Thomas J. *To End All Wars: Woodrow Wilson and the Quest for a New World Order.* New York: Oxford University Press, 1992.

MacMillan, Margaret. *Paris 1919: Six Months That Changed the World.* New York: Random House, 2001.

Mazower, Mark. "Two Cheers for Versailles." *History Today,* July 1999, pp. 8–14.

McDonough, Frank. *The Origins of the First and Second World Wars.* Cambridge, United Kingdom: Cambridge University Press, 1997.

Mee, Charles L., Jr. *The End of Order: Versailles 1919.* New York: E.P. Dutton, 1980.

Prior, Robin, Trevor Wilson, and John Keegan. *The First World War.* London: Cassell, 1999.

Sharp, Alan. *The Versailles Settlement: Peacemaking in Paris, 1919.* New York: St. Martin's Press, 1991.

FURTHER RESOURCES

Brezina, Corona. *The Treaty of Versailles, 1919: A Primary Source Examination of the Treaty That Ended World War I.* New York: Rosen, 2006.

Grant, Reg. *Armistice 1918.* Austin, Tex.: Raintree Steck-Vaughn, 2001.

Hays, Jeff, ed. *The Treaty of Versailles.* San Diego: Greenhaven, 2001.

Rogers, James T. *Woodrow Wilson: Visionary for Peace.* New York: Facts on File, 1997.

Ross, Stewart. *World War I.* Austin, Tex.: Raintree Steck-Vaughn, 1998.

"The Treaty of Versailles, 1919." *Cobblestone*, March 1998. (Entire issue is on treaty.)

WEB SITES

First World War: A Multimedia History of World War One
http://www.firstworldwar.com

The Great War: Evaluating the Treaty of Versailles
http://edsitement.neh.gov/view_lesson_plan.asp?id=424

The Paris Peace Conference and the Treaty of Versailles: The Remaking of Europe in 1919
http://www.ctevans.net/Versailles/Index.html

The Treaty of Versailles
http://www.colby.edu/personal/r/rmscheck/GermanyD1.html

28 June, 1919: The Peace Treaty of Versailles
http://net.lib.byu.edu/~rdh7/wwi/versailles.html

PICTURE CREDITS

INDEX

ABOUT THE AUTHOR

LOUISE CHIPLEY SLAVICEK received her master's degree in American history from the University of Connecticut. She is the author of numerous articles on American and world history for scholarly journals and young people's magazines, including *Cobblestone, Calliope,* and *Highlights for Children.* Her books for young people include *Life Among the Puritans, Women of the American Revolution, Israel, Mao Zedong, The Great Wall of China,* and *Daniel Inouye.*